MW01488696

THE RISE AND FALL OF A SANDCASTLE

What it takes to create and build a thriving company

Taylor, I wrote this book for you and your kind. May you be valiant in battle. And from my heart, thank you Mason for your support and friendship. You are truly missed.

TABLE OF CONTENTS

INTRODUCTION

There is only one first kiss, I am sure you remember yours. That first kiss takes strategy, risk, involves a whole bunch of emotion, and is certainly a learning process. So was creating and building Performance Composites. For me, it was my first kiss with business.

Writing this book captured 15 years of countless events, filled with both internal and external battles, lessons learned, knowledge gained, and principals grasped. I have taken these principals and distilled them into a shot glass of short stories.

I tried to knit them together seamlessly and carry a common theme through the entire writing. However business is not clean, it is not seamless and there is no common theme. Business is a compilation of many ingredients that are incorporated in varying measures under disjointed circumstances.

I have great love, respect and admiration for those who step into entrepreneurship. My hope is these perspectives will help you avoid some of the pitfalls I encountered and enjoy some of the same victories I did.

I continue today in a new adventure, with new men who are conquering a new industry and loving every minute of it. Writing this book helped me to reflect and hold fast to those techniques that I gained through my first kiss. Hopefully yours will be as memorable and enjoyable as mine was.

CHAPTER 1

BUILDING CASTLES IN THE SAND

Business owners are like little kids going to the beach, resource in hand: Shovel? Check. Bucket? Check. Rake? Check. We plop down in the sand with focus and determination and begin building!

Some kids have a plan, some don't. Others have help from family members (investors) others start with nothing. Some share the project with friends or siblings, others prefer to work alone. Some build really extravagant structures, others are rather pedestrian.

In the end all sandcastles seem to succumb to one of these fates:

1. **Kids get discouraged, distracted or run out of time and the project fails before completion.**
2. **There is a fight between the partners and they destroy the project probably at the climatic point.**
3. **Workers go on strike and choose to go swimming rather than build the sandcastle.**
4. **Some big kid (conglomerate) comes in and stomps all over your castle and takes your space.**
5. **You finish creating your sandcastle and it looks awesome!** You leave to go home satisfied. What you don't know is that over time the tides of mother nature will erode your castle and return it to the beach it was before, leaving the sand for the next child to build his great castle creation.

Name one business from the Roman era that is still in existence today. One of the greatest countries ever, with incredible businesses, none survived. Name five in existence from 200 years ago and you will have a very difficult time. Many governments do not last that long.

The business which I created at age 20 lasted until I was 35. Hardly the sustaining force that I thought it would be. However the values gained are an investment that will last a lifetime.

About five years after Janelle and I got married we built a nice home out on two acres in the country. It was a corner lot in a neighborhood with only 20 lots in it. Our lot backed up to 40 acres which made it feel like there was nobody else around. Separating our property from the 40 acres is a pond, which my kids and I use regularly to pitch rocks into. Behind the pond is a large stony and wooded hill which fills the landscape.

One afternoon my son Will and I were out gathering rocks in our yard and throwing them into the pond. He was almost three years old at the time so we stayed around a small patch of dirt not too far off our back porch.

Will was crouched over at the knees, his little hands sifting through the hard clay for small pebbles. I heard him mumble something which I didn't understand so I asked him to repeat it. To this day I can still see him straighten his body, look at me and state "Daddy, these are hard times".

To him they probably were hard times. Here his little patch of dirt was nearly void of pebbles because we had already spent the afternoon collecting them.

When he said it, I started laughing and pondering simultaneously, because behind the pond was the hill with enough stone to fill the pond four times over! The difficult times were only his perspective of the situation, not the reality he lived in.

This conversation between Will and me found new meaning as I walked out of my beloved business, final paycheck in hand, in December 2005. I was the one staring at stripped land now. I had removed all the pebbles from the small patch of clay through 15 years of business dealings. I needed to look up and see the mountain on the other side of the pond and realize that although this business patch was empty, I had a whole world in front of me waiting to be conquered.

This book is about the journey of discovering life lessons learned and perspectives gained that would become the building blocks for my next venture. I've written this for entrepreneurs and those who wish to become one. It is a book that I hope will help form your perspectives on where you are today as well as where you may be heading.

THE GREAT IDEA

Do you remember your original "great idea" and how you protected and nurtured it? As you look back now, what percentage of importance do you think that idea had in the overall success of your venture?

I certainly remember my first great idea. I had forgotten about it for approximately 25 years until my grandmother produced and returned the original contract to me.

At the time of the contract signing I can guess by my hand writing that I was approximately eight years old. Our families would all meet at Grandma's house in the summer for the cousins to reunite and play. As any little boy I loved playing with trucks, specifically semi trucks. Grandpa had the big metal ones that we could load and unload. We would set up certain routes for the trucks to run and deliver goods to pretend stores.

Somehow that "great idea" light bulb flashed for the very first time. I decided to start a trucking company! My Grandpa sold

life insurance and he had very important letterhead for writing
letters. Surely this parchment would be sufficient to make my
new venture official. But before writing the contract I needed an
employee.

One of my younger cousins, Nobel, was playing trucks with me
so I asked if he was interested in driving a truck for my new company when we were big enough. Nobel complied with my request
so I headed off to Grandpa's desk, pulled out one of his official
looking pieces of letterhead and a blue ink pen to start drafting in
cursive.

The contract was simple, in actuality it was more of a decree.
I was forming a trucking company, of which I would be the president and Nobel would drive the truck. Nobel was forced to sign
the document, which obviously brought legitimacy to the venture. With the idea birthed and contract signed, we went back to
playing trucks and I forgot about the great idea for a quarter of a
century.

People have three general misconceptions about business
ideas:

1. **Great ideas are rare.** Great ideas, in fact, are common. Original ideas? Now those are rare. Normally when
people think of something that is original to them, they as-
sume it's great and that it's never been done.

2. **Few people have great ideas.** We think just because
we have great ideas that it automatically means others do not.
Having great ideas is actually very common, most people
have them.

3. **The core value of business is in the quality of the
idea.** Great ideas do not make you a great business person
or even a person with any business acumen at all.

My love for motorcycling and performance drove me to the first real "great idea" of my business career.

Performance Composites Incorporated (PCI) became a manufacturer of high performance products for the motorcycle and automotive industry. Our products were manufactured from composite materials such as Carbon Fiber and Kevlar, which reduce weight, and add strength to vehicles. These components were seen as "jewelry" for the vehicle owner and were market drivers in aesthetic design as well as functional application. PCI supplied high volume private label products to OEM manufacturers such as Yamaha Motor Corporation and Triumph Motorcycles, and a myriad of aftermarket company's world wide.

The core of my original business model was to market products directly to the end user to build our brand image. As PCI grew, it went through three or four distinct phases of change, none of them ever brought us to the point that we executed the exact original business model. In other words success was not necessarily found in the core of the original great idea; success was a byproduct of pursuing it.

Phase One – We intended to develop the complete composite exhaust system in stages. In the first stage we developed the silencer housing. Because we were overextended and needed to generate cash flow we marketed these "composite sleeves" as private label products to other performance companies to generate cash flow. We were a private label product manufacturer who sold business to business. That is much different than the original intention.

Phase Two – Selling the "composite sleeves" worked so well that we captured about 80% of the market and couldn't enter the marketplace with our own product because our clients would have become our competition. We abandoned the original idea of product branding and redefined who we were as a private label manufacturer of composite products for the motorcycle industry. We began developing other composite products, unrelated to exhaust systems such as bodywork and other aesthetic products, which we could sell through our business to business client base. We were diversifying our product range.

Phase Three - This worked well and we began to expand outside the motorcycle industry as a manufacturer of private label composite products. We entered the automotive industry on a small scale. We also developed other products like airboat propeller blades, bicycle parts, and other unrelated products.

As you can see the end result of PCI was entirely different than the core concept or "great idea". The great idea was only important in that it stimulated me to pursue business. The productivity was a byproduct of the great idea, not a direct result from executing it perfectly.

Everyone has ideas and almost everyone has great ideas. People who are willing to give their lives to the pursuit of proving their ideas and bringing them to reality are extremely rare. It is rare to find people who put quality strategy to their ideas and then have the fortitude and commitment to execute them. Very few step out in faith to pursue an idea, even fewer become successful.

In the end though, our rigidity to adhering to a certain "idea" can actually impede reaching true success. One can never derive their identity or measure of success by how closely the original model was executed.

I meet so many people who have their own revolutionary ideas. They guard it like hidden pirate treasure. Somehow they feel like God slighted them by supplying such a great idea without a clear cut path to success. Truth is, it takes a combination of these three ingredients working together to make a concept a cash flowing entity.

Idea

Plan

Execute

Ideas do not have to be great to make a great business. Can you make a great hamburger on the grill? Well, if you can then why don't you have a business bigger than McDonalds! The quality of the business is not found in the originality of the idea, it's found in the planning and execution of the idea.

Many people move directly from the idea or concept stage, directly to the execution stage, without developing any framework for the process of actually doing what they want to do. This, inevitably creates a big mess because the process has not been given consideration, and work is overlooked or mismanaged. If you do not have the patience to properly plan for your idea, you most likely will not have the patience to stick it out and make it great when things get difficult.

There is also the failure to execute which impedes success. I remember late in the life of PCI, I had investigated some new applications for our manufacturing process and technology. Developing a carbon fiber push rod for engines became a viable application. The idea was followed by a planning stage. We found several other patents that had similar technology. We moved forward with the design phase and moved into testing prototypes. The product worked extremely well and patents were filed. It was time to move into the distribution phase.

I made trips to companies like Harley Davidson where our product was tested and reviewed in product planning meetings. Trip after trip, meeting after meeting but the contract did not come. Unfortunately, we encountered a phase in business where we had to return to manufacturing our core products and relocate the facility to Mexico in a cost down measure. This placed the push rod technology on the back burner, and we never returned to pursuing distribution. Great idea, great plan, failure to execute. I often think of the invested time and money, the patent with my name on it, and how ironic that it never produced because I didn't bring it to the finish line of idea, plan, execution.

A business is conceived when the idea is mixed with an executable plan and harnessed with enough fortitude to see it through to positive cash flow. In the end what people need to understand is that the smallest amount of value should be placed on the idea, more value should be placed on the strategy and the highest value placed on the execution necessary to bring it to pass. This is the value system I live by and I often remind myself that the profits ultimately lie in the execution, not in the idea or the strategy.

CHAPTER 3

PERCEPTION AND REALITY

I t's interesting how people perceive business-ownership will be. I'm not talking about the glorious dream of rolling around in some nice rig and having the big house and stature in the community. Or the pure passion you have for your product, people or whatever. It's never as it seems.

My wife, Janelle, and I perform pre-marriage and marriage counseling. One of the things that we believe is God's joke on humanity is what we call "idealistic distortion". In essence it's the rose colored glasses people tend to view the marriage relationship through prior to entering into that union. We administer a test which measures the idealistic distortion people have prior to marriage, which allows us to better understand their perceptions.

Couples come in for their first meeting answering questions with statements such as "nothing could ever cause me to doubt my love for my mate" or "this is the only person in the world I could be happy with." Obviously these answers are not true and they reflect idealistic distortion.

When we begin to dialogue with couples during counseling I purposefully comment that with over three billion people of the opposite gender, you should be able to find another whom is compatible. Thus dispelling the myth, "this is the only person I could be happy with." I also bring out the scenario of one person catching the other in a sultry, adulterous affair, which would indeed cause one to question their love for the other.

The point I aim to communicate is that experiences in life feel differently going through them than they appear from the outside. When watching football, and I have been known to watch my fair share, we read the game completely differently than we would if we were the quarterback on the field. For instance, you are sitting in your lounge chair, window open, cool fall breeze coming in your living room. You have some sort of cheddar snack in your lap, the remote in one hand, cold beverage in the other. As you watch the game you are viewing from 30 different camera angles, seeing all sorts of replays and listening to professional commentary. We usually form our opinion on what we would have done, after the play has ended.

Conversely, the quarterback on the field has 11 hostile men facing him who want to break him into little pieces and 70,000 people yelling at him to personally fail. He gets to view the entire sequence of events from his two eyes looking through a barred helmet with limited vision, no cameras. He is processing what he is seeing through a body which most likely has some sort of pain disrupting his thought process, along with the background noise he has to block out. Topping it off, there are ten men in his huddle looking to him for leadership.

As he approaches the line, his chest is heaving from running around the last few plays, and he is thirsty. His nose is blowing snot bubbles as he is trying to instruct his people, yelling side to side at the line of scrimmage.

Once he starts the play, he has approximately two or three seconds to look down field and find one open receiver out of four men running different routes, while running for his life from defenders and stepping around blocking linemen. When he does make a throw he must thread it into a window approximately two feet by two feet and will probably be leveled regardless of whether the pass is completed or not by that oncoming defensive lineman. He is then expected to get back up and be successful the very next play. This is much different to making decisions from your arm-chair. Things feel differently living through real-time situations then they do from a distance and with the luxury of a time-delay.

When deciding to start a business most people have only experienced an armchair view of what it's like. Maybe they've seen a friend or family member who has achieved some level of success. They see the respect this person receives, the car they drive and the house they live in. They sense this person has more freedom because they are the boss and therefore have the autonomy to do what they want when they want it. There is an assumed access to more money and higher pay scales than jobs working for others. All of these factors usually give people "idealistic distortion" when considering starting a business.

A few years ago some college-aged guys wanted me to play tackle football with them. All were real athletes, with about 2% body fat and ran like gazelles. I, on the other hand have moves like a garbage truck and seemed to have lost all muscle mass from sitting in a chair. But it sounded like a fun way to spend a Satur-day morning, so I loaded up my two sons and went to the football field.

After actually making a few respectable plays and feeling like a part of the group, I decided to go across the middle for a pass. It seemed like a nanosecond after the ball was in my hands that a train ran into my left side. I could hear the ribs cracking like kindling wood. I laid there for a while just taking inventory of my body parts making sure I was still alive and breathing. Our expectations of a moment and the reality of that moment are never one-in-the-same. The experience I had was actually much different than my expectation for the event. I can assure you, whatever expectation you have for business, the actual event will be much different.

At the age of 20 I started writing my first business plan. I had no idea what I was getting myself into. I had grown up with a deep love for motorcycling and wanted to create a performance product company in the power sports industry.

As any green entrepreneur would do, I wrote a naïve plan, expecting everything to go perfectly. Not that I have become negative through business experience, I just look at things differently, knowing that business is executed in an imperfect world. Things don't always go as planned. Any good quarterback will make his reads down-field, but when that defensive back is closing, he looks for his safety-valve tight end and gets rid of the ball. Experience can bring some clarity to how situations feel. But in the end, it's not about things going right or wrong, it's about navigating the unexpected. Your preparation and commitment to dealing with the unexpected is paramount.

My business model had no contingencies for product development ending later or costing more than projected. There were no back-up plans for delays from suppliers during production. I didn't include a time-line for how long it would take to find, hire and train good employees. I certainly didn't have the foresight to plan for performance below what I had forecasted. I didn't even consider such basic issues because I had never been through the experience. Entrepreneurship was still a fairytale concept to me. I made my budget and timeline based on everything going perfectly – which meant on time and at maximum efficiency.

When I finally met the man who would invest in my business model, we had many discussions about the "what ifs". I remember thinking, "I can't believe how pessimistic this guys is, he just thinks the sky is falling." Traits you must learn are to adapt, improvise and overcome.

I didn't realize my future partner had been through his share of wars. He lost one business due to too much growth, another with a bad partnership, and then he battled it out in the steel industry year after year to make a dime, finally selling out in his early 50's. He knew the right questions to ask and where to look for hidden snares.

One of my early goals was to take a company public. I may one day achieve this goal but it is no longer a "must do" in business. I have been fortunate to have friendships with three men who have all taken companies public or run a public company. One failed, one achieved success and sold out, and the third is still running a tough business today.

I sought council from all three men concerning the processes and true day-to-day issues of running a publicly traded company. I now understand the price paid is hardly worth the glory or money that may or may not be earned. The CEO of a publicly traded company never receives mercy, never gets a mulligan and must perform quarter after quarter. No mistakes are allowed.

We have all seen the statistics about business failures, something like 9 out of 10 fail in the first 12 months. My perspective has always been that business is not that tough. People fail because they don't properly plan and they don't know what they are getting into. People step out of the preverbal arm chair into the game and it feels different. They are unprepared for what it actually entails and eventually raise the white flag saying "this isn't what I expected business to be like."

Nevertheless people continue to see or read about the "highlights" of another's business adventures but don't take into account all of the elements that go into producing the victory. Outsiders don't realize the long nights, stress, employee issues, customer and partner relationships which need to be managed, etc. My suggestion is to sit down and discuss with some business owners the reality of ownership. Hopefully the council you receive will be honest and unfettered.

CHAPTER 4

RAISING MONEY

Business is usually a blend of science and art, quantifiable data and intuition mixed together to create something productive. Raising money is no different. Although I believe raising money requires more of the "art" or the intrinsic ingredient than science.

The only portion of business which cannot be boiled down to a specific list of executable tasks is fundraising. This is what separates entrepreneurs from pure corporate types. Entrepreneurs have to see something which does not exist and formulate a plan to create it. They must properly articulate that plan to people, some of whom will hopefully believe him or her and then invest precious start-up funds.

This is a ridiculous paradox of events but somehow, myself included, entrepreneurs are drawn to step into the line of fire with each new passion-filled concept.

I remember when I first started raising money -- I was scared out of my mind. I hated networking and presenting. I hated the way it felt when someone said "hell no!" and I heard it often.

I was completely unqualified and unfit to manage a business when I first started raising money for PCI. I hadn't finished college (barely started!). I had no real experience in my field of interest, I was a poor writer and an even worse communicator. The no's came very easily.

But I wasn't a quitter.

During that time in my life from 20 to 22 years old, I hardly had two nickels to rub together. I started a small roofing business out of necessity which helped me gain my first pieces of business acumen. I operated this business during the two years it took me to fundraise for PCI. It was a great maturing process.

I learned two key factors during this time period:

1.   **There is no limit to the amount of time it can take you to raise money.** PCI fundraising lasted two years, other ventures were much quicker and others, well, I am still pursuing.

2.   **There is no specific formula or pattern for finding your investor.** There are insane stories about how people meet investors. You just have to get after it.

For me it was quite interesting. By this time I had been pitching my business model for about 18 months to anyone who would listen. I had a friend who was a security guard at a local outdoor mall. One evening an older gentlemen came screaming through the parking lot on his son's motorcycle. My friend promptly stopped him for questioning. He learned the older gentlemen, Joey, was trying to "blow out the cobwebs" on his son's motorcycle. My friend told him that I might be able to help him get his motorcycle set up for racing, Joey called me.

When Joey arrived at my house with his motorcycles we struck up a friendship. Over time I presented my business model to him and I can remember his answer like it was yesterday. "Well, no, I am not interested but I do know a guy who might be."

I had heard this 100 times before and knew it was the easy way for someone to let me down. I didn't give it much thought until he called me a few days later and said he had arranged a meeting for me with a man who owned a steel company.

I remember driving out to John's massive company one evening in my old Nissan pick up, different front clip than the back, and mix and match tires. I think one of the windows wouldn't roll up. It couldn't have been a more humble entrance unless I had borrowed a donkey.

That evening I presented John with the information. He felt my energy and realized that I really believed that I could pull this off. We discussed the business model for a few weeks, he asked for prototype parts and reviewed them. We discussed more. Finally he gave me the verdict, "not interested". I was heartbroken, back to roofing.

That autumn I received a promising offer from a businessman in Florida, who was in a similar industry. He was very interested in the concepts and was already working within the composites industry. He informed me verbally that he would be willing to invest in the business model if I would move to Florida. I quickly closed my roofing business and moved with a few thousand dollars in hand.

I spent two months working at his facility, never receiving a dime, a contract or an incorporation. I don't place the blame on him but on myself for being naive to believe him and stay put at his facility working for no money. Finally I was broke and had to go home, with, of course, his promise that he would indeed one day fund the project.

John and I had developed a friendship and kept in touch throughout this and I called him upon my return. He asked me to meet with him and his son for lunch a few weeks after arriving home. After lunch he told me they were willing to invest the money if I still wanted it. One month later we were incorporated and the money was in the bank. Entrepreneurs must be willing to endure the race, until you get the prize of investment capital. This is not the end, it is only the beginning.

Over time I noticed a pattern that evolved in fundraising. It was not a system of just networking, networking, networking, until you meet the right person. Although I preach it's all about percentages in business management, filling the pipeline during fundraising is not the most important thing when looking for investment.

People see when you are drilling for money. It removes much of the trust factor between entrepreneurs and investors which makes the deal much more difficult. It also reflects that you may not care about the investor, just what they invest. This is where ethical problems arise. You must care about the people who entrust their resource to you. Understanding these principles for fundraising will make the experience more fulfilling for you and the investor:

Their money represents their life. They have traded time, effort, security, resource, and talent in exchange for their money. Entrusting their money to me means entrusting a portion of their life.

I care more about seeing my investors receive a return than I do myself. I take pride in knowing those who have invested money with me make money. I don't value my time and money over other people's time and money. People respect that. It makes things much easier if things don't go as planned.

It is a lot easier in the future to raise funds if you have a strong success rate for generating a return. For me though, it is a pride issue. What kind of business guy are you if you raise money for all kinds of businesses and none ever produce for the investor? When my investors get a return it means I was right! I love proving all those people wrong who would not invest with me. It's one of the most enjoyable aspects of generating profits is seeing my investors get their share and those who wouldn't invest left out.

I have never pitched to people I had no relationship with. It might have been a short relationship but I always had enough interaction to learn about their families, their business experience, their personal net worth, their aspirations for investing and future dreams.

There have been times when people wanted to invest with me and I didn't take their money because I didn't think it was the best fit for them or me. I thought about whether I would make the investment in my business if I was in their shoes. Why take the money if they are going to regret it.

I have never taken enough money to bankrupt the investor if the business failed. Start up businesses are risky propositions. Asking someone other than you to invest their life savings is haphazard.

I need to like the investor. Would I enjoy talking to them on the phone and having them stop by my office? Never take money from people you don't feel comfortable with, even when desperate. You are creating a distraction that sacrifices long term peace for short term gains. I work with people I interact with easily.

Through the fundraising process I have never applied undue pressure to close. I want people to fully understand the investment and understand the risk factors. I am not soft closing, but I am not manipulating people into closing a deal. I present the investment, followed up in a direct manner but I never leveraged anyone to buy in.

People primarily invest money in the entrepreneur rather than the business model. The investment is made in the belief that you, the entrepreneur, can execute what you have presented.

CHAPTER 5

DO WHAT YOU DON'T WANT TO DO

Much of success is not dependant on being the smartest, most articulate or even the most prepared. As I have built businesses, and observed friends as well, many times it boils down to doing what others are unwilling to do. To the one who is willing comes the prize of victory.

Once PCI was funded, I was the only employee, and had the entire responsibility of developing products. My partners had invested in a concept and now it was time to bring the concept to reality -- and then get it to market. I had approximately four months to accomplish this before we ran out of money and the business would close.

There was a lot of excitement during this time for me. I was bringing in equipment, building out the offices and formally establishing our company. I had pursued financing for two years and it was such a relief to actually have raised the money. I felt a certain sense of relief. There were many late nights filled with positive emotions during the pursuit of production.

As the clock ticked I felt the emotions change. There were now new pressures to perform as the timeline condensed. Money and time both became scarce. Our product development was showing promise, we were getting close with the process and product quality, but it was beginning to create frustration. My partners began leaning on me for answers. We needed more money and time.

I convinced them to double the investment and give me another 60 days. They saw progress and obliged. This additional investment definitely raised the pressure to perform. I had approximately 30 days left, we were so close to making the product market acceptable but I couldn't get it over the hump. My partner was now discussing the liquidation process at the end of the month. His displeasure in my perceived failure was very clear.

I exhausted every resource I had to make the product market acceptable and became frustrated, depressed, confused and angry. I had a choice to make every day that I went into work. I could go through the motions, take the path of least resistance, ride out the last 30 days and call it quits -- or I could keep working.

My days and nights consisted of modifying tooling, keeping meticulous records for experiments dealing with chemical mixtures, materials, cure cycle times and temperatures. I spent many nights setting a walk-in oven at 100 degrees and sleeping on the floor for two or three hours while parts were cycling.

I remember one day in particular at 2a.m., I was wearing a nice shirt that I had recently purchased, which was stupid on my part. I spilled some chemicals on myself ruining my clothes. I just sat on the floor and leaned against a freezer and thought "can anything go right for me at all?" I wanted to quit, but honestly I trusted that God Himself hadn't brought me to this point just to see me fail. This was not some cruel joke, it was life and if I wanted to be successful I needed to accept the reality of the situation and keep moving forward with confidence. Obviously I hadn't counted on this when I wrote my business plan.

I chose to work through my emotions and continue trying to solve the impossible. I believe that many businesses fail because people don't want to face the reality of the situation. They choose to deny the real problems or issues and take the path of least resistance.

My choice to battle through finally paid off. A sales representative from a materials company stopped by out of the blue, with approximately two weeks left on my clock. He thought he had the chemicals that would fix my issue, some special chemicals which were left over from a proprietary aircraft project. He hustled off, only to return a few hours later with fresh materials to try. That night I had my first market-acceptable part in hand, which I sent to our potential clients.

Within a week we had a hand written purchase order from the owner of the largest company in our industry! They were in a bind and needed product desperately. We were now the only company within the USA with the technology to supply them immediately. I had gone from hated to celebrated with my partners.

We were now hiring employees, entering production and shipping product. It was another exciting time in business. We were moving forward. I have learned that overcoming one obstacle does not result in lush green pastures. My business career has continually consisted of making myself do what I didn't want to do, whether out of necessity or for growth. I am personally willing to endure to get to the prize on the other side, it's well worth the sacrifice.

CHAPTER

BARRIERS

It took about six months to complete the development process and begin production. We had received a large blanket-order for parts, with a weekly delivery schedule which stretched over many months. We geared up to meet current production demands as well as build in capacity to meet future orders that we were forecasting.

The very first week of production we shipped 52 parts. Our team of three had killed themselves to get these hand-made components finished, packaged and ready to ship. On Friday we celebrated with drinks while gathered around the lone 24" cubed box containing the result from all our efforts, waiting for UPS to ship them off to the new owner. Later that night I reviewed our outstanding orders. I faced the realization that 52 pieces per week would not satisfy the demand and definitely not cover the overhead.

I had to quickly embrace the production volume required to

meet demand. Creating a realistic structure that would yield what we needed was necessary. I had to figure out how we could increase our productivity -- and the answer wasn't found in a text book. I then had to convince our personnel that it could be done. Time was a luxury we couldn't afford because people wanted our products and they wanted them now. All of this needed to be addressed by Monday morning.

The following week we set the production schedule for 100. There was a backlash from our new employees that the number couldn't be achieved. We adjusted steps within the production model, created some efficiencies and BAM! -we were at 72 pieces. The third week we broke 100.

As the months rolled forward and turned into years, demand rose to unbelievable levels, and we continued to diligently work at finding new ways to organize and process workflow. Production went from 52 components per week to over 2,000 components per week at our zenith.

Through the entire process we continually confronted our mental barrier. As the leader I had to find a quantifiable way through the barrier and effectively communicate to the employees that it was possible. That belief would unify us into a team which could then attack the issues we faced. Think about these statements for a moment:

1. **Just because we haven't done it doesn't mean it can't be done.**
2. **Just because the way we tried didn't work, doesn't mean there isn't another way which does work.**
3. **Just because this is our maximum output today, doesn't mean it's the max output we will ever achieve.**
4. **Just because we don't have the answer today doesn't mean that the answer does not exist.**

We all face barriers that keep us from progressing both personally and organizationally. It's not whether the barrier exists it's the belief that the barrier can be eliminated. If you don't believe you can break a barrier, you never will. Believing you can overcome it dramatically increases your chances for success.

There are generally two types of thinkers: agnostic and visionary. Agnostic is the most common. Agnostic thinkers need to see that it can be done before they believe they can do it. Visionary people can perceive the unseen, and it appears to be attainable to them. A leader is challenged with convincing others not only that a feat can be accomplished – but also that they are the ones who can do it.

The first barrier that must be removed in order to run a successful business is doubt in what can be accomplished. Once you believe that you can overcome obstacles, the answer of how will be found easily.

CHAPTER

7

SOME DOGS DON'T HUNT

D o you know what the difference is between a hunting dog and a dog that can hunt? Just because you are bred to be a hunting dog, doesn't mean you can hunt.

You will learn the difference between the two once you take them into the wilderness and release them to track game. Some hunting dogs, once turned lose, will get on the scent of their prey, trail it for a while, but become distracted as they cross scents for other animals.

Imagine being in the woods, you release your Black and Tan to trail a bear. He runs through the woods baying for a while, until he crosses a rabbit scent. He diverts and heads off in a new direction, scrambles around for a while, then crosses a deer scent, which he hurriedly picks up and follows. This routine lasts all day but produces only frustration for the hunter because no game is delivered.

Inevitably this type of hunting dog never succeeds, because

they continually get distracted before the pursuit is over. Hunting dogs that cannot hunt are those which follow every scent that comes along. Dogs that can hunt stay on the scent until they produce a kill. They are disciplined and do not get distracted as they cross other scents, focused only on producing game for the hunter.

When I was 15-years-old a man at our church bought me a Beagle puppy as a gift. Beagles are bred to hunt rabbits but they don't come out of the womb ready without training. I had an uncle who owned a kennel and trained hunting dogs in the state of Washington. I called him to ask how to start "training" a dog to follow a scent.

I took Nipper through a series of training events. The first step consisted of rubbing a piece of hot dog across the kitchen floor to create a scent trail, leaving the piece of food at the end. Slowly he learned to follow the scent, rewarded with a piece of hot dog at the end of the trail. We graduated to rubbing the hot dogs through the dirt. Soon enough he became adept enough to follow these scents through all kinds of terrain.

One of the issues that most young entrepreneurs face are distractions disguised as opportunity. Many times after beginning to generate cash flow, there is a rush as you hit a vein of new ideas and concepts for cash generation. These opportunities can become distractions from building a strong business foundation.

When Performance Composites was a young and growing company, I felt that we could build anything out of composite materials. However, there was an overconfidence that blinded the better judgment of decision making . Therefore, we set off to develop a range of products and probably wasted precious resource at the onset of our business.

Fortunately I had a partner who knew better. John asked me one afternoon if I knew the difference between a hunting dog and a dog that could hunt. I didn't know the difference but he did. Over time he brought correction and guidance which helped me to stay focused on the elementary building blocks of a business. When the timing was right, defined by profitability, we diversified.

Entrepreneurs, including me, traditionally have a short attention span. My young company needed to be focused on expanding our distribution network for the current products, developing systems and staff, and cost-down measures on the manufacturing side. These steps would further strengthen the company rather than bleeding precious resource and diverting attention to new products so early on within the embryonic stage of the company.

There are some entrepreneurs which follow every scent they pick up in the wind, always chasing the next great idea. There are others who stay on the scent, even in those times of opportunistic distraction. Develop discipline and learn to finish what you start in life. Allowing every wind of opportunity to guide your life mostly ends in frustration and disappointment. My suggestion is to stay the course until what you are pursuing produces, it usually pays off better than jumping scents.

CHAPTER 8

THREE CORE ELEMENTS

I loved cars and motorcycles growing up. I imagined myself cruising in that muscle car or racing Motocross on some tricked out motorcycle. Most of my time was spent planning how I was going to get those things and how I'd fix them. Inevitably it always came down to whether I could buy it, fix it up, enjoy it, sell it for a profit and reinvest in something bigger and better. It was more about the strategy and execution than it was the actual vehicle and lifestyle.

My sophomore year in high school I had been keeping my eye on the newspaper to buy my first motorcycle. I was fifteen at the time and was in love with the idea of racing Motocross. I wanted to ride and race more than my next breath of air but the dream was out of reach because of money.

During the previous school year I had worked raking leaves, shoveling snow, moving lawns and throwing newspapers to get enough money saved up to buy a basket case motorcycle. One afternoon, while hanging out playing video games, a buddy told me he had a friend who had two dirt bikes in his barn which were for sale at $100 each. He was already 16 and had a pickup and drivers license so we loaded up and drove to his friend's house in the country. I still remember going into the kid's barn and seeing a pile of parts -- frame here, wheels there, engine completely torn apart and in boxes. "I'll take it!" I exclaimed.

That summer I spent in my basement and garage rebuilding the motorcycle. My dad had absolutely no mechanical skill beyond cussing at the parts for me when things got frustrating. Our next door neighbor, who was an aircraft engine mechanic, was recruited to help me. He would sneak out of his house in the evening and come down to our basement. My dad would give him a Pabst Blue Ribbon which he would sip while he taught me about rebuilding engines. Gene would continually teach me, "To get an engine to run there are three basic things you must have; compression, spark, and fuel." Compression, spark and fuel, if you have those three ingredients you can make an engine run.

Over the years even when working on race teams or my own million dollar motorcycle development project, it always came back to compression, spark and fuel. If you are in Formula 1 at the pinnacle of racing and are working for Ferrari, it still comes down to compression, spark and fuel. The fact of the matter is these ingredients never change.

We worked all summer long to get the Yamaha rebuilt and I remember the first time I fired it up in the back yard and rode it around with sheer excitement. It smoked like a chimney but it ran. I had so much fun I ran into the pole holding my dad's porch up and almost knocked it down.

Years into my first business I realized through a chain of

events that getting a business to produce was much the same way. There are always three core ingredients which you must have to get your business to generate cash flow.

Supply Chain

Internal Management

Distribution Network

Study these until they are burned into your brain. They are the core elements of any cash flowing business. If you can't understand this, you will never be able to make a business generate cash flow.

SUPPLY CHAIN

The origin of where your goods and services are produced whether inside or outside your company. Without, this element, whatever that looks like, you would not have a product or service to sell.

INTERNAL MANAGEMENT

This defines the organization, the systems, the arrangement of human resource within your company and how it is structured to create and maintain profitability.

DISTRIBUTION NETWORK

The external mechanisms or channels used by your organization to get your goods and services into the hands of your clients.

Recounting the early days of PCI, it's very clear these three raw elements come together and produce cash flow.

As discussed briefly earlier, to get our product produced I had to build the initial supply chain for raw materials which we created our products from. But it wasn't the only thing I had to do. I couldn't focus solely on this, spending all my time attempting to make the supply chain perfect, therefore making the product perfect. Initially we made our product just good enough for the market first, and focused simultaneously on the other two ingredients.

Internal management had to be created to actually operate the other two ends of supply and distribution. Obviously our systems, human resource, and working capital were miniscule during start up, but there was a framework that was developed and implemented.

In addition we had to start creating the distribution network. I spent time marketing our product to build a client base. Sounds simple enough but many people focus only on their product which reflects their great idea. Unfortunately people attach their identity to the idea or product and the balance of the business suffers.

In essence, I see the supply chain as an extension cord that's plugged into the wall, the distribution network is like a power tool, internal management must connect the two so that power flows from the source and makes the tool run. I have boiled my career down to plugging in extension cords, through good internal management connecting supply chains to distribution networks.

Once cash flow was generated, we could go back and modify the three ingredients to improve the company quality and efficiency therefore increasing the profitability and strength of the company. Some of the ingredients I enjoyed working on more than others, however I had to discipline myself to become educated and proficient in all three. The success of the business is always a reflection of the owner's ability to improve these three areas.

The reason that I stress this so much is that many entrepreneurs have talent in one area and neglect the other two. We want to focus on what we enjoy rather than focusing on what is necessary to make the business profitable. Your focus during start up should be on all three ingredients simultaneously. Without all three functioning at some level you will never ever generate cash flow.

Once a business is mature people can lose sight of the crucial importance of each core ingredient. Losing any of these ingredients will cause catastrophic failure. It is imperative, no matter how large or complex your organization becomes, you cannot ever lose sight of your supply chain, internal management or distribution network.

Over the course of time we upgraded and refined our supply chain, internal management and our distribution network. Unproductive clients were dropped and productive client relationships were groomed. Suppliers were replaced and raw materials were refined. Internal process systems and human resource were developed, all simultaneously. We made the business engine run at its maximum efficiency at PCI. It was very satisfying in my twenties to experience the same feelings I did at 15 when my motorcycle was up and running -- and running very well.

CHAPTER

HOW TO PLAY CHESS

When I was about ten-years-old I learned how to play chess at elementary school. My dad was a college professor but had never learned how to play chess, so the son became the teacher. There were books at school with strategies in them and I memorized the moves before coming home to play chess with dad.

Continually I would bait him into moves and the strategies worked, I always won and he was certainly frustrated. Over time, my dad figured out these patterns and began to change his reactions. My strategies stopped working and I began to lose.

At this point I had to begin "projecting" the game and learn how to anticipate his next few moves, or combination of next few moves. I had to make a few different short term strategies, which one I used was determined by his response to my actions. The end goal stayed the same, but as the board was rearranged and my resource of pieces changed the strategy evolved with it. Throughout any given game, the short term strategy could change many times, just to survive and try to achieve the unvarying end goal.

There is another type of business experience that begins to occur sometime within the first few years of being in business. Shortly after generating a profit we start to feel really good about ourselves and our accomplishment but it was not time to relax.

Markets are organic and they continue to change. The business environment may be somewhat different from when you wrote your business model. There may be developing pressures from foreign suppliers, massive companies diluting the market, local competition from other business, or products and services may become less relevant.

Market adaptation becomes the first pruning in business. We have growth, but need to prune the inefficiencies. Strategy must change. General outlines of plans are usually much better than strict strategic objectives because the market and culture we live in is very fluid today.

This was very difficult for me to learn because if I had any one natural skill it might have been as a strategist. I made very complex plans and became very frustrated if things didn't go exactly as planned. As I matured my outlook on strategic planning changed and I developed a handy framework for continual development:

Gather

Sift

Plan

Execute

We gather information from internal and external sources

about our business, market, people, systems, and products, etc. Information gathering is an ongoing process that is part of the fabric of your life.

This information must be sifted to separate the noise from what is usable data. There is an overload of data in our world. Identify what is important to strategic planning and disregard the rest.

A plan or framework is developed from the usable information gathered. Your original plans should go through regular modification. This is not haphazard, it should be scheduled and integrated into your management routine. Don't let the distractions of running day to day operations keep you from continually modifying your strategic plans.

Execute your plans. This is always the most important phase of planning. Why do I consider execution part of the planning phase? The execution phase proves whether your information gathering, assessment and planning was effective. Without execution you will never know if your process for planning works. Prove it!

Gather, sift, plan and execute is a repeatable cycle that I use for continually managing our strategic framework. The cycle of planning and implementation is an ongoing process that is a key aspect of managerial duty and cannot be overlooked.

Early in my career I graded my success at how well we conformed to a long term strategy. Now I realize success is found in how well we can adapt to changing markets.

- **Make a loose framework which holds your core guideposts for direction of long term planning, between three and five years.**
- Do not make finite and detailed plans that extend longer than one year.
- Evaluate and update your framework at least twice per year. Encapsulate this in an executive summary for review once executed.
- Revisit finite plans quarterly for adjustments during execution.

Business is much like playing chess, you can usually calculate 2 or 3 moves ahead but you can't forecast the whole game. Why not? Because you aren't sure what moves the other player will make. In business you are not certain what decisions other companies, markets or cultures will make and how they will affect your future strategy.

The most effective strategist is one who can make executable plans based on a mixture of quantifiable data and intuition but have the confidence and flexibility to adapt the plan to a changing culture.

CHAPTER 10

RUN IT LIKE IT'S A FIVE MILLION DOLLAR COMPANY

We were about two years into our business and annual revenue was running about a half million dollars. I felt like we were working crazy hours and still having issues coming up. There was definitely a demand for our products. We had found a niche and were exploiting it. However, there were problems internally, little holes in the ship which kept us from rising with the tide. I knew that small holes would eventually sink a big ship, so they needed to be addressed.

I was having a conversation with a friend who owned a marketing company. He was preparing some marketing materials for an upcoming trade show for us and I was in the process of proofing them. As we were reviewing the materials I was describing the issues we were having.

"Eric, where do you want your company to be?" he asked.

My personal goal had always been $5 million annually. His response changed the way I studied business form then on.

"If that's what you want to be, then start running this like it's a five million dollar company right now."

I believe business owners often get stuck in the rut of how they have always done things. They don't see the need to change with a "what's the use" attitude. Maybe I might not have been so eager for change if I was 40-years-old, but I was only 24 and I took it as a personal challenge.

I embarked on studying what systems, leadership techniques, and other organizational structures would help me run my business like a $5 million dollar company. I spent about two years learning, working, teaching and building our company structure. We didn't reach $5 million revenue in that two years but we did reach $2 million, which was excellent growth for our market.

Even though the sales were there, had we not made the changes and tried to inject the growth, it would have toppled the business. Had we not accepted the challenge and adapted our company to handle the sales increase, we could have opened the door to strengthening the competition.

A necessary part of our survival was learning to manage ourselves like a much larger organization. Immediately it didn't make a difference, over the long haul it did. Looking back it didn't give us an immediate gain, because the changes took time. However it did allow for exponential growth over the next few years. It gave us the capacity to grow and manage the growth. We were planning ahead and building the company to handle the growth we were expecting some years down the road.

What I learned through this process is that there are two kinds of people, some are proactive and others are reactive. I am a proactive person because I want to stay ahead of the curve. If I wait to react until things are broken, the issues become catastrophic. Had I waited to build the company to produce three times the product until the orders were in hand, it would have been too late.

Visualize what you want your organization to be and begin to develop all areas to reflect what you want. Set specific milestones based on another organization or components of other organizations that you want in yours. Quantify exactly what you see and what benefits you expect to gain. Change doesn't happen overnight, it's always incremental. A persistent commitment to positive change will no doubt bring it into existence.

CHAPTER 11

SELLING ON VALUE

People buy products based on the perceived value they get in exchange for their hard-earned cash. We used to set up lemonade stands in the summer time as kids. The town we lived in was a small college town with cottage-like neighborhoods. People walked everywhere.

The summer time was always a good time for a glass of lemonade. But there were factors that affected whether people really wanted our product. What was the price? Well, if it was low enough that people could pull out change from their pocket, there was a good chance they would invest. Asking for a dollar was like asking a stranger to pay our college tuition - no way! But a dime or quarter was always greeted with friendliness and an exchange.

The quality of our product was also important. Only Kool-Aid products were sold and proudly displayed at our stands. Whether we realized it or not, kids associated "cool" with Kool-Aid.

Finally we had to serve people well. On those hot days people would stream by our stand but nobody wanted to stop if there was a line. Pouring the drinks quickly (without spilling) became an important step in the execution of the lemonade stand.

Price, service and quality are the three elements that make up "value". It is critical that you address all three elements when you market your products.

Value = Price + Service + Quality

Evaluating your customers during conversation leads to identifying what their "value button" is. Although all people buy on price, service and quality, people value these components at different rates. Engaging in conversation will help to find their value button and enable you to properly present your products or services based on their need.

As PCI continued to expand we entered the European market for product distribution. We did not open an office overseas as that would have been cost prohibitive. As we began marketing our products I had to evaluate whether price, service or quality was the hot button.

We found that our quality exceeded that which our overseas competitors produced. The Euro market looked at their components as replaceable rather than a lifetime product as the US market did. We produced lifetime products for the US market which made our technology an upgrade to European customers. Although our product was superior this was not enough to get our new potential clients off the fence.

Pricing was definitely in our favor. The dollar was very weak compared to the Euro and British Pound which allowed us to make good margins while still giving a good price to our clients.

This still wasn't enough to motivate a sale.

The fact we are thousands of miles away on the other side of the Atlantic was the problem. We were unknown and that created fear in their camp. It wasn't easy for clients to pick up the phone and say, "I need 1,000 pieces in two weeks" and have the confidence we would deliver. Service was the issue and we had to address it. I realized we needed to make them feel like we were right next door and that we could handle their needs.

The service button was the hot button for our potential Euro clients. I needed to push their button and close the deal on value of price, quality and service. Here is how we chose to break down the barrier.

- **We created marketing materials where they could see our facility, staff, quality control process and products.** This was done on an interactive DVD which we sent to people. Our potential clients now had faces with names, an understanding of processes, and a general view of who we were. We were people not just a Web site.
- **I traveled a lot.** I was at their facility, integrating with their staff and building relationships. I provided an attitude of service and willingness to do whatever it took to garner their trust. We worked issues out together at their office, not over the phone or internet.
- **The key was figuring out how to get the clients product quickly.** I had to be able to deliver the product as quickly, as a local supplier. We negotiated special volume air freight rates with BAX Global and lowered our price to offset the additional shipping charges.

In the end, the total combination of price, quality and service opened the door east of the Atlantic and allowed PCI to double our sales and diversify our client base very rapidly. Without understanding the importance of knowing how our clients valued price, service and quality PCI would never have broken into the European market.

12

RESPONSIBILITY

My dad and I watched a lot of westerns when I was young. It had been many years since I had seen a good western, until "3:10 to Yuma" came out. It reminded me of how clearly responsibility was outlined within those outlaw groups. There was usually the preverbal line in the sand, and if you crossed it? Well, you got shot. I like that simple management style because everyone knows what is expected and what the consequences are if not achieved.

I really like people and care about them deeply. Some of my previous employees may beg to differ but I am confident the fruit thus far from my business career reflects an owner who may be firm but also cares about people and their wellbeing.

There have been plenty of times I have loaned or given away piles of cash, or vehicles, rented apartments for people, counseled them through family issues, supported through addictions, and the list goes on. But there is a line in the sand which I clearly use as a compass. I understand where my real responsibility begins and ends with employees.

In small business one of the most difficult issues we face is managing the relationship between employer and employee. What we need to clearly communicate is the responsibility both parties have to the company. This healthy conjunctive relationship is what produces results within an organization. Here is the line in the sand.

> **RESPONSIBILITY OF THE EMPLOYER**
> Provide opportunity and resource for the employee to complete the work outlined.
>
> **RESPONSIBILITY OF THE EMPLOYEE**
> Complete the outlined work in the agreed time for the agreed pay.

I developed a reputation early on for firing people. Not a very good reputation nevertheless one that has stayed with me. I have never had a problem firing someone who did not fulfill their responsibility. Conversely I have never fired anyone who has fulfilled their responsibility.

I have always seen my responsibility as an employer as one who provides opportunity and resource for people to advance in life and fulfill the obligation they have committed themselves to within our organization. Sometimes employees fail to meet expectations voluntarily. I am, at some level offended that they were unwilling to fulfill their obligation when they clearly told me they would at the time of hiring.

The commitment to the organization is the common bond

employer and employees should have.

Obviously there must be some grace given during the developmental process. But at some point in the not too distant future people must produce that which they were hired for.

An inability to fire people that do not fulfill their obligation seriously undermines any authority you expect to hold with your employees. It builds a culture of acceptance for poor performance, regardless of your words. Empty words and threats erode your company like waves on a sandy beach.

Poor performance is like a virus, it can spread from person to person. Do yourself a favor and cut those under producing leeches. Don't fool yourself into believing they are really committed to you or your organization or to you. Commitment is measured by production.

13

IT'S LIKE AN ORCHESTRA

As any red blooded American male teenager thinks at some point, I realized it must be my calling to play guitar in a rock band. Somewhere around 14-years-old I got the gear, the lessons and the tablatures and started playing.

Things changed dramatically a few years later when some buddies and I got together and tried to actually play as a band. It was a complete disaster. It finally occurred to me that it was very difficult to get everyone playing together to actually sound good. The guitar was abandoned but the hair stayed long.

Building a business out of people is much like putting an orchestra together. You are the conductor but it never starts with picking up the baton and waving it around with great music emitting from the band.

In actuality it starts with teaching people to play an instrument and how to read music. People have to learn the basics. The difficulty comes in trying to get everyone to play in harmony.

That is exactly what an organization is, it's coordinated decisions and actions from a group of people to achieve a common goal. If you are the CEO then you are nothing more than the one who conducts the music. If you are an entrepreneur then you probably had to learn every instrument, and play them all simultaneously, then train others one at a time to play some of the instruments as you handed off duties.

Every business I've ever built has been this way. You start alone, build a small team, systems, procedures, train, refine, and hire more. But there are stages or barriers that must be crossed. We always had to build the profitability high enough, or cash flow strong enough to hire and train the new staff. Harmony must again be achieved between the people on staff, which equates to profitability. There is an ebb and flow, where you build, stretch and max yourself out. Once you reach and maintain a certain level of efficiency, then you can hire, train, relax and do it again.

Every time we grow, we introduce some level of inefficiency; this is expected. But our responsibility is to teach people and improve the systems until harmony is again restored and greater profits are achieved. Once that happens you have the green light to move forward again.

If you feel like you're playing three instruments at once and trying to direct others, you are not alone. This is the plight of all small businesses. But don't lose hope, find a way to hire others and teach them to play, even if it's frustrating at first. They may not play the instrument as well as you in the beginning so give them a chance to learn, be a patient teacher.

The growth of your company is dependant on your ability to continually replace yourself as you build your organization beneath you. But you must continually maintain harmony between all the human components within your organization. If the harmony remains you will continue to be successful, if it fades, your business will become a house of cards.

THE CATALYST

As a leader, one of the most difficult tasks is stimulating growth while maintaining unity. Early on I learned that it was difficult for people to do things they felt was beyond their ability, or to bring change in areas of comfort. There were times when I knew we needed to expand our production capacity or improve our quality but needed to avoid the "us and them" mentality that could develop between my office and the production staff.

Typically any change is received with resistance from employees. Naturally employees feel management is always working them harder, demanding higher levels of quality and efficiency. How much juice can we squeeze from the lemon? It doesn't matter how we wrap the package of change, it always feels like the ivory tower has sent down the next requirement for the little people to carry out. This is the heart of the "us and them" mentality which exists in many organizations.

The source and premise of the directive determines whether

it can be inflammatory. Altering the origin and purpose of the change can stimulate positive results without creating a conflict. In order to continue the unity between myself and our employees, I had to create external pressure for change. This also unified us as a team and accomplished the goal of producing increase.

If a directive comes from the market rather than your office, the boss remains on the "us" side and the external force becomes "them". The key is finding a way to create and harness external pressure to unify your organization and stimulate the changes needed.

During most of my career I stimulated growth by engaging new business. If we were trying to increase our capacity, why not increase the orders first? This translated into us working together to increase our capacity after the orders came in rather than me demanding a voluntary increase in capacity to further expand our sales. The sales came first, followed by the capacity increase.

Obviously, this creates heavy risk in that a failure to produce and meet the demand can cause a loss of clients and damage to your organizations image. However the reward is multifaceted.

Increasing demand from an external source allows us to accomplish the following:

- **There is unification between management and employees.** Management is now receiving as much pressure as the employees. This results in bonding with employees to work collectively and implement necessary changes to win the battle together.
- **You are leveraging an outside source to create discomfort within your organization.** That discomfort will drive people to accept the need for change. The need for change is much less acceptable when people are in a comfortable place.
- **This gives you an opportunity to implement systems** or structural changes within your organization that have been previously developed, with less resistance from personnel.

We want growth. But we need to retain unification through the uncomfortable process of change. Harnessing external pressures is a good way to drive unification and change together.

CHAPTER 15

THE GOLDEN RULE

When I hired people and we would begin indoctrinating them into our culture through a comprehensive training process. There were no junk rules and regulations. I had hired this person and hoped my judgment was good. It was time to trust them and treat them like an adult, not micromanage them. During the training phase of the employee I always made the one and only rule crystal clear. Nothing else matters if this rule is disregarded. It is the only rule we would live by.

Do what's in the best interest of the company.

The process of business is a series of decisions and actions based on available information. Those coordinated actions by multiple people make up the organization. The unknown lies in understanding what the intention was behind people's decisions.

Intentions can range widely, this variance can effect the over-all quality and performance of a company. For instance if your controller does not enjoy collecting money because they must confront people on the phone, they may subconsciously always stay busy to avoid doing that part of their job. In turn that slows down cash flow.

In addition I believe most people have good intentions we just have to give the correct intention to them. Everything in life teaches that mistakes are bad and that we are penalized for making them. However to me, mistakes are acceptable, as long as you learn from them and implement corrective measures to keep them from happening again.

Generally people are afraid of making mistakes because they don't want to get in trouble with their boss. They avoid situations where issues can arise. Traditionally when people make mistakes the natural reaction is to cover them up. Employers now become investigators attempting to get details to draw conclusions. In essence this negative philosophy keeps organizations from pro-gressing.

I worked very hard with our managers at PCI to build a corpo-rate trust between them and myself and each other. We all en-counter situations which we have not faced in the past. A unique set of circumstance arise for various reasons and a decision has to be made. You certainly don't want every decision coming to your office so we empower people to make decisions in the best inter-est of our organization. However, that does not automatically mean things will turn out ok. If they don't turn out successfully I want that manager to be confident that we are on the same team and I won't lop an arm off if it goes south.

I wanted to remove the fear from making bad decisions, create trust and improve communication so people will make decisions in the moment without regard. We want our managers making decisions! Once people begin to make decisions, I can coach and develop their decision making process to reflect the philosophy we want.

Typically, if a decision creates a negative result I would want to sit down with the manager and discuss their thought process behind the decision. Why would that decision reflect the best interest of our company? We then refine their thinking process, put in a corrective measure and move on.

If you make a mistake and can show me why you were attempting to do what was in the company's best interest -- no problem. Mistakes are not bad, we learn from them. Mistakes made while trying to improve the company, those are always forgiven. If you make mistakes and it's clear your interests lie in other areas rather than our company, I'll just replace you.

An example would be a marketing person developing some electronic media and the campaign fails. Your reaction should be "why did you think this campaign was best to reach our customer and why was this particular method best for our company?" At that point it's a team effort between you and your manager to troubleshoot the issue together and develop a resolution that is best for the company, which they can then implement. Hopefully they will leave the meeting with a more refined decision making process and the next time will produce better results.

Often when we hire new managers they aren't adept to our culture. They stop by my office and explain a situation they are facing, obviously looking for direction on how to handle the matter. I will listen and simply ask them, "What do you think is in the best interest of the company?" It's interesting to hear them dialogue about their perspective and the conversation usually ends with building their confidence for decision making.

We landed a contract for body parts with Triumph Motorcycles. The part was complex in comparison to the standard products we manufactured. Weekly volume deliveries were high from the start but, unfortunately, the development process did not translate over to production.

One of the production managers chose to run full production to fill the orders although we were losing money on the shipments. I questioned him about this and his feeling was that it was better to maintain the client's production in the short term as he was confident they would find a solution rather quickly. His opinion was that the value of the client was more important than the short term financial loss and that was in the best interest of the company.

It's a motto which I continually reinforce in word and action, even if it means personal sacrifice. We must all remember that the entity, our company, must be healthy for all of us to remain employed and prospering. Keeping this company healthy and growing is paramount. I am here to benefit the company first and from the company increase I am benefited.

What we have overlooked is that employees need a filter to send all decisions through. You can't regulate every situation with a manual, and you certainly can't expect people to remember everything written in one. For me, I like things simple and boiled it down to one statement. When you make a decision, do what's in the best interest of the company. You do that, whether right or wrong, I'll respect it.

CHAPTER 16

SYSTEMS AND HOW TO USE THEM

A few years ago we got a new DVR system for our television. Of course I unboxed all the goodies, and recognized most of them. Included was the big silver box which was the DVR, there was the cord with the yellow, red and white ends, some other small parts probably optional in my mind, and then there was the manual with the size four font on it, finally a big laminated sheet with color drawings and short sentences.

I set out to try and hook it all up without using any of the directions. I failed miserably and only produced the blue screen. At this point I had to resort to the directions. There was no way I was going to use that big manual, so I reached for the laminated card with color pictures, it was easy to follow and within a few minutes the DVR was working perfectly. I loved the color pictures and short sentences on the laminated card. I hated the tiny black text translated into three languages, because it was too confusing and overwhelming.

The key to systems is building one which people will use. I believe people develop very elaborate systems, which do the job to the nth degree but the employees don't execute because they are either too complex or too time consuming.

Typically the person who develops the system takes pride in the complexity, thinking somehow that it reflects their personal abilities. However if people won't use it, the system is worthless. Think about it, which tools do you use the most in your toolbox, the crescent wrench. Why? Because it's versatile and easy to use. Our systems should not be a reflection of complexity to flex our muscles, they should be simple tools we use to improve the productivity within the organization.

I was always looking for ways to increase quality and efficiency in manufacturing. We finally ended up with a very simple system that evolved into something very effective over time.

The ingredients were the following:

- **A bonus which would be paid at the end of each quarter.** We bid in 10% waste in all our products. If our production department ran less than 10%, we rewarded them with ½ of the savings. If they saved the company $20,000 we split $10,000 between everyone in production. The production manager got an extra 10% for carrying the responsibility.

- **They had to manufacture a minimum number of parts per man hour worked**, which kept the efficiency side in check. We would log the percent of waste and the parts per man hour produced weekly. Each day as the parts were stored on racks, we recorded the data on simple spreadsheets.
- **This was then reported to the production department on a "golf card" at the end of each week.** The golf card showed total hours worked, total parts, waste percentage and parts per man hour worked. These four elements easily described their productivity and efficiency.

Each week we would add the score, showing how much money each group was up or down for the quarter. We had three production teams and it even became competitive between the shifts.

This system worked great and some shifts received healthy bonuses. However if a production team started out badly at the beginning of the quarter, they would quit trying to reach the bonus. This had a detrimental effect on the company and could offset the gains realized by the other shifts.

What we needed was something which would hold their focus and keep them pushing from week to week. If they started out poorly, we needed them to continue trying and not quit. We instituted an additional bonus, for hitting the weekly goals, regardless of their performance recorded from other weeks within the same quarter. So for each good week they received a spiff of some type.

The monetary compensation for just one week was not great, so we tried to spruce the program by giving dinner gift cards, movie passes and other small rewards. These were received with mixed results.

Not giving up on the plan I asked myself what were these men interested in? It was pretty easy to see by the shirts, hats and talk they were all into car racing. I found a go-kart track a few miles from our facility and went to check it out.

The track was a road race style course with a banked wall at one end where the karts would reach speeds between 50 and 60 miles per hour. At an inch off the ground I know it would feel like you were going 200 miles-per-hour!

The next week I took all our employees to the track where we had a practice session and then a 30 minute race. In 15 years of business I have never seen anything as effective as what we did with the karting.

All our guys wanted to talk about was the last race and the next one coming up. It had an incredible galvanizing effect on our people. In fact they really lost site of the quarterly bonus and were much more focused on the weekly race Friday afternoon.

The weekly karting ensured us of reaching the bonus quarterly and effectively managing our waste below the levels bid into the parts. The reason for this was the weekly karting was much more important to them than the bonus at the end of the quarter. This kept their focus very detailed throughout their hours at work.

We eventually developed a points series and had a champion-ship in the fall and spring. One of the things I miss most is the competition and comradery we developed every Friday. I found myself being even more involved because I wanted to help them achieve the goal so we could all go race. Yes, I raced too and the employees loved it.

In conclusion we had many systems which ran our company,

the above was just one example. Here are my golden rules for systems:

1. **Systems must be very easy for everyone to use.**
2. **The system must produce the results that you want.**
3. **Make sure everyone buys into the system.**

The key objective was to put the accountability at the employee level for quality and efficiency. The primary objective was to remove barriers between the front office and production. This was another step toward unification by passing the responsibility for quality and efficiency directly to the employees.

CHAPTER 17

TRUE GRIT

D o you have the real grit to fight it out in the trenches? What you read about at 30,000 feet has to be executed at 2am on the production floor and 7am in the office.

For me, the internal battle has always been more challenging than the external battle. I have learned that if I can win the battle mentally, I can execute. Everyone has limiting thoughts and feelings. And it's not a one time battle that we face, win, and it's all green pastures on the other side. It's more like going on a strenuous hike through the woods, climbing over rocks, wading through streams, and then reaching a clearing for a short period of time before heading back into the woods again.

Life is a continual cycle in battling thoughts and feelings; it's not a one-battle war. This isn't a two hour movie which builds to a crescendo, and the hero rides into the sunset with the girl. Owning a business is a day-in and day-out battle. By winning internal and external battles daily, we can make major progress.

Starting off I felt that others were better, smarter, more talented and more charismatic than me. The theory has always been that successful people are more talented people. In my opinion we all have the natural ingredients to be successful. Determination to press through adversity seems to be a better measuring stick for success than talent alone.

When you start something in life, finish it. Be careful about the things you engage in, and choose them wisely. Don't acclimate yourself to starting things you don't complete, for this is quitting. I grew up hearing my dad say "winners never quit and quitters never win."

Choose to engage in things you are willing to see through until it's a victory. If it's unworthy of your commitment to complete, it's not worth pursuing.

CHAPTER 18

THE INTANGIBLES

Y ou know the people I'm talking about, don't you? Those people who have that "it" factor. It's not something you acquire by studying in school or working out in the weight room. It's an ingredient within a person that seems to give them superhuman abilities in very specific situations. It's definitely a gift from God, and although not something we can create in people it is something we can develop.

There are all kinds of people who have that intangible ingredient in their field of expertise. Cooks who prepare food with a pinch of this and a shot of that while never using a recipe. Mechanics who can listen to an engine with no diagnostic equipment and know exactly what's wrong. Those who trade in the stock market and intuitively know which way it's going most of the time. Teachers, who read their students, and know how to motivate each and every one of them in unique ways. Pastors, who can preach a perfect message and compel people, without ever using notes.

Successful organizations have certain intangibles working within them. Over the years I compiled a list of intangible characteristics. If my organization had these intangibles I felt like we would be successful. For the organization to have them, the people had to have them. My mission was to find people who encompassed these characteristics, hire and develop them, and align the organization around these qualities.

Three ingredients became paramount for human resource to function well together and be productive. It became even more critical when we moved our manufacturing to Mexico, due to the language and cultural barriers.

The "it" factor for organizations is summed up in three ingredients:

Communication
Problem Solving
Teamwork

The departments which make up a business do not function independently, rather they are all interdependent. Employees typically view their area's performance in an independent way, without considering the adverse effects their decisions make on other areas. Many times decisions are made for individual department gain while a counteracting loss is caused in others. When this occurs, the organization can not grow as a whole.

An engine is similar to an organization. It is made up of many different components, pistons, cam shafts, valves, electronics, etc. These components make up the sum, which produces horsepower. This horsepower is measured on a machine called a dynamometer.

The dynamometer is like a balance sheet. You can see the gains and losses from your decisions very easily.

I always loved working with engines because I was intrigued by how changing one component would affect the whole sum. I learned that changing any one component had an effect, positive or negative, on all other components. When making a decision to change any one component, the effects on all other components must first be calculated.

Today I love business for the same reason, only now I am working with people who have independent thought processes, emotions, dreams and desires. The interplay between human beings is much more dramatic than working with inanimate objects. There must be a common set of ingredients between the diversity of people and for me it is communication, problem solving and team. Using this knowledge I can choose to build the organization around the commonality of these traits.

Communication, problem solving and teamwork are our initial ingredients. Through these ingredients, the individual components of an organization improve their own efficiency, consider the effects they have on other components, and calculate ways to minimize collateral damage.

COMMUNICATION

Isn't this what we need as business owners? People who can describe what they experience within their work world are invaluable to entrepreneurs. They may see and understand a lot, but if they can't properly articulate it, the information is useless.

How people describe what they see: their experiences, their perspectives, are part of what makes up your information gathering system. Lack of information or misinformation from employees usually makes for bad decisions by management.

Great racing motorcycles are developed because the test riders are great communicators about what is happening to the vehicle on a test track. If the riders can't convey the positive and negative changes to the engineering staff, the test drive is pointless.

I was in England for a test session during a motorcycle development exercise. A private track had been rented and the test session kept secret from the media. Engineers from all over Europe had flown in to give support to the test rider for two days. The progress of the team would be easily measured by decreasing lap times over the course of the test session.

It was June, but the weather is always cool in England. The skies were partly cloudy and all the plants were lush and green. The track's asphalt wound through rolling hills and into a long straight by the paddock area.

When I arrived, the championship winning rider was napping on a picnic table. Engineers were humming, talking in low tones while mechanics made final preparations for the first test session.

The lead engineer was introduced to the rider. The total sum of the events would come down to two factors, would the lead engineer ask the test rider the right questions and would the test rider be able to articulate the correct answers.

From the outside looking in people would think the session's most important ingredients would be the equipment available, the number of personnel, track conditions -- in essence the tangibles. However, the intangible ingredient of communication between these two men who hardly knew one another determined the outcome.

Sessions were run again and again, with changes being made between each outing. At the end of an adjustment the rider would take the motorcycle out for some hard laps. Quantifiable data would be recorded from the on-board computer as well as lap times. But the most important part was what the test rider communicated to the lead engineer and how the lead engineer processed those comments into mechanical changes to the vehicle. Communication was also vitally important between the lead engineer and the other mechanics and engineers on staff.

During the first day there were nearly a dozen outings with mechanical adjustments between each round. That evening as we drove back to the hotel, I was watching video footage on the camera. There was a particularly technical portion of the track where the rider was navigating a set of turns and elevation changes all in about 1 ½ seconds. I asked him what was happening at this section. He talked for several minutes about every detail of what was happening with his body, mind and the motorcycle.

I was amazed at his ability to find so much valuable information from such a short period of time and to communicate it clearly to the engineers so they could make the proper adjustments, which was reflected in improved lap times. This was the main contributing factor to the success of the tests. All the money, time and hard work invested in making changes would have been worthless unless the test rider could properly articulate what happened with the motorcycle in 1 ½ second increments to an engineer.

The supply of good information between departments always improves efficiency and productivity. The better the information is and the faster the transmittal between departments translates to bigger gains in faster growth.

PROBLEM SOLVING

Problem solving, in my estimation, is the most important element in building a business. Every day we encounter a flurry of issues which were unexpected, or outside of our normal boundaries of thought and action. For instance, how do you raise investment capital, or develop the next great product, create that new management system and so on. Problem solving is what makes up much of our daily lives, it breeds increased efficiencies and productivity. Problem solving is what we need in our employees and from ourselves.

I was in my office one day when I received an unexpected phone call. It was right after our stock sale and I had been flying high on the success we had experienced. Life had been good, very good. But this phone call quickly caused me to lower the landing gear and get back to work.

Our largest customer had called and explained that one of our silencer housings had failed structurally. A man riding a motorcycle in Europe had the back end of his silencer blow off like a cannon. Fortunately, there were no cars or pedestrians behind him who would've been injured by receiving the speeding hot metal object.

There were hasty demands made, a threat of a recall, damages, his voice faded out as I began to think how we were going to address the issue.

I met with one of the greatest problem solvers I've ever known, and one of my closest friends. A composites engineer who had worked for British Aerospace, designed F1 cars and done many other cool things I only dreamed about.

Kevin worked for the company who supplied the materials we manufactured the housings from. I called, he agreed to an impromptu meeting. Very Kevin like to set his schedule aside and say "come on over."

I explained the issue with fast hand gestures, and fragmented sentences as the stress oozed from me. Shortly he had me calmed down and we began to look at the issue analytically.

Was the issue a failure on our part, or was it another component in the system. Did it have to do with assembly process? Could the end user have modified the components which caused the failure? There were seemingly endless options; multiple components to blame. The actual cause of failure, the correct answer, would have to be found before the solution could be developed to correct it.

The next day I was on a plane to LA. The customer and I would meet, review the damaged goods and begin putting a plan of action together.

Within 24 hours I was in a board room looking at my shredded carbon fiber silencer housing. It was a delicate situation because there were multiple dynamics playing out. If I found issues with the clients components and assembly methods, would I appear to just be shifting the blame and escaping liability. If that happened would I lose the client? If we accepted responsibility would it cost us everything?

Our process worked as follows: we manufactured and shipped the carbon fiber housings to our client, who drilled holes in the ends of the housing and attached metal components. The metal end cap that was attached by rivets had blown off. The rivet bodies had torn through the carbon fiber under pressure like a knife through butter. It clearly looked like our product had failed, plain and simple.

However on closer inspection other issues surfaced. The

rivet holes were not drilled a distance equally from the end of
the sleeve. Some were closer than others. The rivet material was
aluminum and it seemed distorted from the heat that had been
generated inside the silencer.

I asked to see their assembly process. What we found were
men drilling the housings on a machine but without a fixture.
This caused an irregular hole pattern. More thoughts flooded my
mind, we had never set a standard for minimum distance between
the hole and end of the housing. Another trip to Kevin's office
was necessary.

So there Kevin and I sat, sipping PG Tips and looking at parts.
He began teaching me the exponential decline in strength carbon
fiber had when moving the hole incrementally closer to the edge.

At this point I could have blamed the mess on the client, opted
out of any responsibility and been right in the eyes of business.
But we didn't just want to be right. We wanted a solution. We
needed to fix the problem, save the client and our book of business.

Kevin worked for a month in a laboratory testing shear
strengths of rivets, hole sizes, edge distances and the like. We
came up with a new stronger material that, if imbedded into the
sleeve, would help resist the tearing.

I worked on the manufacturing process. I created a drilling
fixture for the client and made samples. With Kevin's report in
hand, samples and fixture in tow I headed back to LA for a presentation and test session.

I presented our findings. Their failed assembly process had
caused the failure. Because the holes were not drilled consistent-
ly, those closest to the edge had failed. Once one failed they went
off like popcorn and the end of the silencer had blown off. The

aluminum rivets were partially to blame as well.

With all that being said I didn't close my briefcase and say goodbye. I presented our improved product which contained new materials to make the ends stronger. I also pulled out the drilling fixture and insisted they use it to keep the hole drilling consistent.

Finally, I presented the mathematical findings from Kevin's report which ended all dispute. We instituted a minimum edge distance the holes could be placed, the correct hole size and also the suggested type of rivet fastener to be used.

This problem solving and implementation improved our relationship with the customer, improved our product, saved the account and avoided the potential liability we faced.

Your organization's ability to improve has to do with how fast you can identify problems, implement solutions and bring positive results. Your ability to hire, teach and empower your employees to problem solve is the key to exponential organizational development.

TEAMWORK

Of what use is a brick. In and of itself not much. They are fire honed chunks of clay shaped into a rectangular block. Great for stubbing a toe if unseen, other than that very little value is found.

But if you take a pile of bricks and stack them orderly great structures can be created. Have you ever been to Rome? I have always enjoyed walking the streets of the old Roman city. It's filled with structures made from stones which are individually worthless but together have created functional style, strength and beauty which have lasted thousands of years.

People have to understand that nothing great is ever done

from complete independentence, even individual sports. Greg Norman had physical trainers, swing coaches, mentors, confidants, cooks, assistants and a battery of people who create and enhance the environment he worked in. He may execute the swings alone but the result of the swing is the compilation of many unseen contributions which account for his physical and mental wellbeing.

Corporations are more like team sports -- and the outcome is even more dependant on good teamwork. The essence of everything we do is team. You must create an environment where people experience and understand team concept, team commitment and team accomplishment.

When we moved our manufacturing operations to Mexico, the most important aspect was building the team and creating the team atmosphere. I didn't do this through traditional team building exercises. We experienced team building exercises every day, the kinds of situations which cause people to advance in a career or lose a job. They were real life situations where clients were gained or lost, profits were achieved or squandered. This was business in the trenches and what better time to learn to shoot a gun than in a firefight?

In Mexico I found the wastelands of top-down management. People seeking primarily to advance themselves rather than advance the organization. People afraid to admit when they had made a mistake because they feared demotion. Nobody wanted to accept responsibility for failure but everyone wanted to take the credit for success. The only thing they were unified in was stonewalling the ownership from America on any pertinent information. I was seen as the enemy, everyone was the enemy.

The team concept didn't exist and we had to create that.

Team development originates with teaching people from basis of humility and transparency. We built trust through rewarding the transparency of those willing to find their mistakes and weed them out. Those who hide mistakes and shifted blame were eliminated.

What came out of the new freedom people experienced was the delight and satisfaction in actually making the organization better. It unified us. Borders melted, people were seen as peers, everyone spoke the same language.

By our fourth month in Mexico the plant had unified and produced 20% more product than our plant did in the United States after 10 years. It was an amazing accomplishment and we shared the victory together. In my mind it was due to the fact we created an environment of trust, which breeds commitment, and produces a team.

Find these intangibles within people, feed them, nourish them, cause them to grow.

Communication
Problem Solving
Teamwork

Foster them within your organization, make them cornerstones of your corporate nature.

CHAPTER 19

LEVERAGE

I remember working for an insulation company one summer with a buddy of mine. It was just after high school graduation. Neither of us were too motivated for anything other than riding motorcycles and having a good time. Working was a means to an end.

On one particular day we were hauling roofing shingles from a jobsite to the public dump. I was driving an old El Camino that was owned by the company and it was straining from the weight we had loaded on its back. Rain had fallen and the ground was soft.

I crept along through the dump looking for a place we could unload. We were laughing and paying little attention to our surroundings when the truck became captive to the red clay. I gunned the engine and promptly buried the truck to its frame.

The day was early and we were sure that after unloading we could drive the old beast to freedom. We unloaded the shingles into a pile not far from the rear of the truck, dug trenches around the tires, and filled them with debris. No luck. Several hours later and after much coaxing we sat on the tailgate, the stubborn old truck unwilling to cooperate.

Once again we evaluated our surroundings and found an old pole about twenty feet long. Somehow we dreamed up a scheme to use the pole as a fulcrum to help spring our steed free. The shingle pile became an important element as the pole was routed over the shingles and under the rear of the truck. More debris was placed under the tires, my buddy gunned the engine as I bounced up and down on the pole. The truck lurched, and finally rocked it's way to freedom!

Our world is in a constant evolutionary process; people, markets, technology, communities, everything. Our ability to recognize and adapt to our surroundings is incredibly important. However, understanding the times we live in isn't enough. The intuitive ability to exploit available elements and create leverage within your market means ultimate victory.

I had intended to build a company that retailed performance products from composite materials. What we found was that the technology was so rare that we could indeed wholesale products to existing performance product companies and gain market share very quickly without building a brand image. That obviously had long term negative implications but initially, due to the lack of competition, we found a niche and could grow very rapidly.

Over time, as competition entered the market, especially from low cost manufacturing countries, we needed to redefine why clients would continue to do business with us. What leverage did we have over our low cost competitors? I sat on the tailgate in my mind evaluating what we had available in our current surroundings.

Having experience within the industry and intimate knowledge of how our clients worked made all the difference for our new found leverage. We knew that companies like Yamaha wanted to sell composite products through their dealerships with their brand name. We also knew that the end user continually demanded the types of products we created. What was the separation between us and overseas suppliers who were less expensive?

The constraint within our client base was time and manpower for product development. There was also a lack of knowledge for developing products from composites. Product managers would apply their staff to develop products where their experience base was, usually metal components.

Our leverage didn't come in the form of lower cost products, faster delivery times or higher quality. We offered to develop products for free. Our company retained the ownership of the tooling and the client agreed to distribute the products through their dealerships.

We would present product ideas and pricing models to our clients. They researched whether the product would sell, and if so, they would send us a vehicle and say "send us some prototypes!" Once the products were developed clients would promote them through print and online media, as well as product reviews and displays at trade shows. We were leveraging their distribution channels.

Our company made an investment in product development without the guarantee of an order at the end. However we knew that once a product entered production, it was highly unlikely for them to switch vendors anywhere along the product life cycle. This service of free product development became our leverage to maintain and enrich relationships with companies like Triumph Motorcycles and Yamaha Motor Corporation.

Ultimately our ability to recognize and adapt to our business surroundings sustained a long and healthy life in the face of continual adverse conditions. There were plenty of times I wanted to kick back, but I knew there were people overseas looking at my market, *my market*, and I had to continually recognize the changes within our industry, find new leverage, and implement adaptation.

CHAPTER

THE GOOD TIMES

And there have been many good times. Classifying "good times" in regards to being in business depends on the rubric used to define 'good.' In my twenties, the lens I used to view success and greatness was much different than the one I use now.

Seeing our products being used by the top professional racing teams, watching riders compete with our product on television and in print. All of these things allowed us to feel accomplished, successful. But this was an emotional "we did it" kind of thing.

We built a state of the art composites manufacturing facility with many additional benefits. I had a motocross track built on the five acres right outside the bay doors. Motorcycle manufacturers were always supplying us with bikes to develop products for. So ride we did. We had plenty of fun in the evenings or off times riding cool motorcycles on our personal track. Sometimes I'd get the production manager out there and just blow off some steam.

There were showers, a kitchen, and a lounge at our facility. I always felt like if we were spending more time there than at our homes it needed to be nice, so it was. I had a huge office with natural hardwoods, a great view with lots of floor to ceiling glass.

We took our managers to Las Vegas every fall for a trade show and to have some fun. It was all part of this adventure we were experiencing.

Our client base was located primarily in LA and Europe. I spent many weeks out of the year flying first class to incredible destinations such as Milan, Munich, London, Paris and many others. It was a normal way of life and one I became accustomed to.

My wife Janelle traveled with me from time to time and we would explore the world. I remember our first wedding anniversary we spent 10 days on the cliffs of the Italian Riviera.

I sold a large portion of my shared in PCI and for the first time in life had a pot of gold to do those things you always wanted to do. I paid cash for my first new car, and then a second six months later. Janelle and I built our dream home. We had money to make other investments, and start other businesses. Having my own capital to invest in new ventures was incredibly stimulating for a budding entrepreneur. I was 29 and was letting the good times roll.

In a period of about seven years I went from pauper to prince. Life was much different, but the external things didn't always tell the whole story. All of these things are real and come with success and you should enjoy them.

Unfortunately when we look at the good times in the future we think they are separate from the bad times, the boring times, the insecure times or the frustrating times. We segment our thoughts into categories. Good times look like this, but bad times look like that.

Success is not the absence of difficulty, which is how we envision it before we get there. What I discovered is that life is full of many contributing factors which are usually experienced simultaneously or in close succession. If you are waiting to measure your success by how easy your life or job is, that time will never come.

For instance, when flying first class I was probably preparing for a presentation, reading financial statements or studying a book, much like the one you are reading, and just trying to get better as a person and as a business owner.

While riding Motocross after work I was problem solving some issue inside my helmet. I would be considering the necessity of firing someone but regretting pulling the trigger. Driving home in my new ride most likely consisted of talking on the phone to clients who have a long list of demands that need immediate attention. And those vacations always consisted of calls from the office with information on the latest production crisis at hand.

Finally as you move up the socioeconomic scale, there is jealousy from family, friends and colleagues. That always changes things. All of these factors can impede your enjoyment of what you have achieved -- if you let them.

The good times are something that unfold like pages in a book. It's not a destination we arrive at one day and say "I made it". It's not measured in what you have or don't have, what pressure is present or absent. Make sure you properly define what success really is before you set out on your journey.

Both the positives and negatives I described are the bi-product of being productive and profitable. Productivity and the bi-products therein are different than the good times. They cannot give you the good times. Anytime in your life can be the good times or the bad times. That's your choice.

CHAPTER 21

CHANGING THE DYNAMICS

There is an ecology that exists within every organization. It's similar to the ecology within a jungle. All creatures must learn to coexist and a balance is found between them. Several factors can impact that ecology.

Adding new creatures changes the structure and dynamics. Think about adding a lion or a snake into an environment where there were none before. The existing creatures need to change and adapt to the new kids on the block. Additionally the lion now has to find his way in an unfamiliar environment for survival.

The removal of creatures from any ecology will inevitably change the life which remains behind. Animals adapt to fill gaps left in the food chain. In other instances the environment itself changes and causes some to become extinct while those who remain must adapt to the new and ever changing world.

Ecology of business organizations carries more value than I

realized when starting PCI. I underestimated the impact that changing the key people (or any people for that matter) would have on our organization.

Changing people changes the dynamics of the relationships within the organization as people realign themselves. It changes the information flow and perspectives behind the information given. It changes how you address conflicts. It changes your ability to execute the strategic plan. All of this effects the bottom line.

Throughout the first seven years of our business we developed an interesting culture. There were three partners, two working and one silent. We also added two more key pieces early on: a production manager and a controller.

Although externally it might not appear that the pieces fit well, we found a way to coexist. A balance was found in how our personalities and skills interacted, which was important in maintaining the company's growth for a long period of time. Fundamentally we had an aligned ideology on what we wanted to accomplish and this helped people to overlook character flaws or personality differences. We had a high amount of trust, and the flow of information maintained a high level of accountability. There were a lot of fun and fulfilling times along the way. We found our places within the jungle we had created.

In 1999 a person was interested in buying into our company. He was what I considered a friend. A man who was self made, a few years older than myself and in a parallel industry. He owned a materials supply company and was looking to diversify. Over the years we had done some business together. Early on we purchased some materials from his organization. I would see him at trade shows and other events where we would spend time together. He had reasons for wanting to buy into our company, some were professional and others were personal.

When Alex bought into our company, he became a working partner. The original silent partner was now gone. Alex's skill set, although it was quality, didn't fit well within our jungle. We had run productively for a long period of time, and now we had introduced a new party into that balanced environment. It felt like we were carrying extra weight.

In an effort to make a good fit, our controller left and we handed those duties over to Alex. His talents were stronger in other areas rather than managing the paperwork for our finances. This created some erosion within our efficiencies as a company while also increasing the cost basis.

When John, the silent partner exited, I lost someone I could confide in. He had been a great mentor and teacher. Although we didn't talk much, when we did it was always impacting for me. I had someone I could be vulnerable with and express the issues I faced in business. He gave good advice.

Alex and I removed James, another year or so later. Now Alex and I were the only two partners, both worked, but it wasn't the same. Two years later our production manager left for another opportunity after a decade of service. Next man up. The culture was continuing to change.

People left, new people were added, some positions were absorbed, job descriptions changed. The market was changing and we had to adapt and overcome new unforeseen issues. Overall the strong ecology we created over the first seven years eroded over the next six.

From my perspective, we had transitioned from a unified force containing trust and accountability to some talented people who didn't fit well together. People were guarded, somewhat untrusting. The information that was communicated between departments was not unfettered. It was jaded, partial information, which was designed to give a certain perspective rather than truthful enough to bring hearty debate.

Trust and accountability build unity. Unity can outweigh pure talent if there is no cohesiveness among the people involved. We lost the underlying ingredient which bound us together, which was "let's work together and get better, stronger, faster," and was replaced with "let's make more money," and "what's in it for me?"

People are attracted to an environment by an underlying philosophy. It exudes throughout every person's thought process and action. People can come and go as long as those core philosophies stay the same. Why? --Because the new people will be attracted as the old ones were. Change the basis for why you do what you do, and it will change the type of people you attract. The ice age hit our jungle.

GOOD FENCES MAKE GOOD NEIGHBORS

When I was about eleven years old my dad purchased a lake house on Lake Shafer in Indiana. It was a very small lake house which we affectionately called the caboose. It only had one large room for living, dining and eating. There was one bedroom and bathroom in the back. Dad didn't buy the property for the house; he bought it for the land and the view.

The lot was densely wooded and overlooked a huge cove. The lot was not at water level. There is a hill, nearly a cliff, about 40 feet high. There were decks, including a tunnel through the cliff from the top to the bottom. There were many mature maple and elm trees providing shade. We had several decks for sunning and a floating island which was great fun for a preteen boy.

The purchase came with one fly in the soup: a bad neighbor. The cottages were close to each other with no fencing between us and them. Their family was much different than ours. There always seemed to be arguing, screaming and banging doors. People were intruding on our privacy and continually placing a damper on the weekend trips.

Finally my dad had enough. He ordered an eight foot high privacy fence and had it installed on the property line. Inside our fence he planted more bushes and trees along with the construction of a shed. All of it helped to separate and protect our weekend objectives from theirs. Life was vastly improved!

One area widely overlooked in start up small business is structuring the contracts between shareholders. Contracts have great value however their benefit is usually misunderstood by entrepreneurs.

A contract will not take a man who lacks integrity and give it to him, nor does it have the power to control one who is unscrupulous. If you believe that the person you are going into business with does not have integrity, just don't do it, regardless of how well the opportunity is framed for you. No contract will insulate you against a lack of character in others.

If your attitude is "well I will just sue him if things go wrong", you have just grabbed the knife by the blade and your enemy holds the other end.

Character in your partner is the cornerstone for a good partnership, not a good contract. Contracts only help to define, positions, roles, contributions and rewards. They help people look into the future and say "what do we do when things are good, when things are bad, how do we resolve core issues that could tear down a company?"

A healthy relationship between partners is reflected in their ability to discuss and define in writing these issues before business has begun. If you are afraid to define the issues before business starts because you don't want to rock the boat, how will you right the ship in a storm?

Usually at the onset of a business relationship, partners are giddy about the possibilities which they can achieve together. There is some "idealistic distortion" which takes place. People choose to minimize the importance of contracts, believing those issues will work themselves out. Many people refuse to even broach the subject and ask for such contracts to be created. In either event without the fences you will inevitably have more issues than you would with them.

If addressing these issues and defining them in a contract destroys the relationship before the business starts, you saved yourself time, money and emotional distress.

WHAT CONTRACTS CANNOT DO
Give people integrity or insulate you from one who has none.

WHAT CONTRACTS CAN DO
Help define boundaries, positions, responsibilities and compensations as well as structure a way to resolve issues in difficult times.

There are a few core agreements that are necessary to structuring your relationship.

OPERATING AGREEMENT

- Defined who has legal position within the company.
- Defines how authority is given to those positions.

SHAREHOLDER AGREEMENT

- Buy / Sell provision; in case one party wants to sell out, or if there needs to be a split due to irreconcilable differences.
- Death provision; outlines if a sale of stock will occur if a party dies and how the stock will be paid for.
- Valuation provision, how the company will be valued annually which supports both the buy/sell and the death provision.
- Non-compete; defines boundaries for partners who split after a disagreement.

EMPLOYEE CONTRACT

- Defines responsibilities for working shareholders, for what they do oversee.
- Defines boundaries within the company for what they do not oversee.

These documents are very important fences and most definitely help to ensure a healthier relationship whether things go very well or very wrong. In either instance whether things go well or poorly, both sets of circumstances can place heavy strain on relationships between partners. I have been through the good and bad times, both creating a unique set of problems for partners and their relationship.

One observation I have made with all my partners, now in four different businesses is that although corporate objectives may be aligned, we always have different personal objectives.

It is impossible for anyone to align personal objectives and keep them aligned through a lifetime. The realization and acceptance of this will bring you to the conclusion that contracts are important to deal with the discrepancies in personal objectives.

Overcome the fear and risk of asking for such documents and get them drafted. They will cause you as partners to consider and discuss many issues which you are avoiding or unaware of. Those issues resolved now, while both parties are willing, will save many headaches down the road of business.

People tend to feel like they are asking for a prenuptial agreement, and treating it like a marriage. It's not marriage and it's not a pre-nup! Businesses are entities that can be bought, sold, traded, and liquidated, wives are not!

When I first started in business with PCI, I had two partners. One partner was silent and in the beginning held the majority of the shares. The other partner and I were working partners and held the minority share. I had legitimate concern about the fact that the other minority working partner was the son of the majority partner. How would I navigate this?

Fortunately my mentor was a fair man and we put in place some framework for stock purchasing, employee compensation based on performance and key man insurance in case of death. The point I want to make is this, we all had difference objectives, but working with men of integrity we were able to work all those details out.

John was probably 50 and had no interest in working in a business like this. He wanted an exit strategy for his stock (return on his investment) and coverage in case of death. I wanted to make sure I had rights to purchase stock, earn more money for running the company if I hit certain milestones, and wanted control.

All of these components worked perfectly. I was motivated to build the business because I knew I would receive certain benefits for my personal contribution as an employee. John followed through and compensated me as planned, which further fueled me. I had milestones for purchasing additional stock, which were executed and provided more control as skills were proven. John was using his exit strategy and it worked as designed.

All of this worked because the men involved had character, discussed it at the beginning of the relationship, and wanted to make it work. I am greatly appreciative to John for guiding us through this process. Although he could have taken advantage of me due to my naivety, he did not. This was truly a reflection of his character which I appreciate deeply. The agreements worked because the people had pure motives and intentions, even when times were difficult.

Seven years into the business I negotiated on behalf of our company with a man who wanted to buy shares in PCI and become a working partner.

The company was valued at approximately 5 times the price to earnings ratio. I had purchased stock along the way and was now cashing in, along with John who was getting out completely; James was taking a small cut and letting his ride.

When Alex bought in we had our attorneys create very comprehensive contracts for employment and shareholder agreements. Everyone felt very comfortable, but the security was deceptive.

One of the most important points of this book is the following; there is a difference between a shareholder and an employee.

The compensation you receive for owning shares is a distribution or dividend, and you receive the percentage of profits equal to the shares you own. An employee is compensated for their level of responsibility and performance.

In football the quarterback usually makes substantially more money than anyone else on the team, yet he is just one of eleven players on the field at any given time. Why do quarterbacks make more money than a tight end? The quarterback touches the ball every play and therefore carries more responsibility.

Most of the issues that I seemed to face in business dealt with the fact that partners produce at different rates, making different contributions of impact for the business. Typically in a partnership there is a primary person and a secondary person. They contribute to the business at different levels, carry differences of responsibility, and therefore should be compensated according to their contribution.

However many partners believe that since they own an equal amount of shares, they should receive an equal amount of payroll. What people must understand is that your stock ownership has nothing to do with the contribution you make as an employee or the compensation you receive from being an employee. Ownership does not give you the right to receive contribution as an employee without fulfilling obligations that position requires.

Being a shareholder who is an employee and does not perform their duties does an injustice to the organization, other partners and real employees.

It undermines the psyche of the primary contributors and creates dissention within the ranks. You may feel like you are getting away with something but in actuality you are unwinding the business. High producers do not stay in environments where others are rewarded for poor performance.

Approximately two years into the new partnership, James' work performance was suffering greatly. The company wasn't making as much money as it had previously because our margins were thinner with the new pressure from China.

In addition he was spending thousands of dollars procuring items we didn't need in an effort to try and carry some level of productivity. James was supposed to manage the tooling department which created the molds we used to make the parts. The department was inefficient, didn't perform and usually items ended up being farmed out due the department's poor performance.

Finally I started documenting the failures according to our employee contract and informing him. We reached a point where Alex and I chose to remove him as an employee. This had no bearing on his position as a shareholder, and we were not looking to remove him from the corporation, just as an employee. There is a difference.

What was in the best interest of the company was to reclaim the salary and benefits we were spending on James and reinvest those in another area. I proceeded to remove James, who was completely cooperative and very helpful in the process. The pressure was high and honestly he was relieved to be out from underneath the anvil.

We must be honest with ourselves and look at our contributions and see if they are commiserate to our salaries, and the same for others within the organization. If partners can get past the pride and actually reward the horses that pull the cart, the company would grow and all the shareholders would be rewarded.

However in a small organization pride is on the line and most people are too insecure to admit when their contribution is less than others.

There is a big difference between being invaluable and having value. I personally do not believe there is a person who is invaluable to any organization however everyone adds value. It's our ability as partners to evaluate the value of each employee, even ourselves as employees and compensate accordingly.

In the end James chose to action his buy/sell and remove himself form the corporation as a shareholder. The contracts had proven effective. All parties worked together.

Contracts can be very difficult to enforce, especially if there are only two partners involved. Do not be deceived into believing that just because you have the contract that it is easy to enforce.

When Alex and I parted ways, my attorney reviewed the claims that I had and advised me in the following way. "Yes these are legitimate claims that you have. However, when this goes to trial there is no guarantee that a jury will side with you. A jury is unpredictable. So plan to invest thousands of dollars and spend the next year pursuing this but there is no guarantee."

Having contracts does not guarantee outcome. It can take years to get a claim resolved, and if it is resolved to your satisfaction, you still have to collect on the judgment. There is a major cost and time investment in the pursuit of enforcing an agreement.

From my perspective, I preferred to go out and make new money, rather than pursuing a claim that I had against my former partner. It was easier for me to start fresh on a new endeavor and allow Alex to do the same.

The best part about contracts is not our ability to enforce

them, rather to use them as fences to separate ourselves, to bring accountability and offer as guideposts. Enforcement is risky but having them may mean you never have to. I believe having them is like having a gun. It can bring some security, but hope to God you never have to use it.

View contracts as a framework for defining outcomes for issues prior to their occurrence. Contracts do not communicate mistrust rather they help improve communication and create safety for the parties involved.

CHAPTER 23

YOU AGAINST THE WORLD

I thought everyone had idealistic views about business. I thought that, in and of itself, business could be enjoyable because everyone came together to do something great as a team, and along the way we could all enjoy the fruit of our labors. This was very naive because, primarily, my idealism is a minority view among most people. Business can become a big money grab, and that realization changes things when you are in it day in and day out as those traits begin to surface in employees, partners, vendors and clients.

I suppose the dark side of business came alive for me not when we were struggling but when we first became successful and had money within the company. People tend to unify during times of crisis, due to fear, but during times of prosperity they can fragment due to greed.

Jealousy began to surface from employees towards owners and

between partners as we became successful. Employees who had been with us didn't like the fact I had a nice office upstairs and out of the way. It was a difficult transition for some to see my career advance.

The perceived prominence I had in the industry didn't sit well with my partners. I took the heat as the front man when things were bad, but I also received a lot of credit when things went well. Everyone thought they deserved more money, more recognition, more authority and it was never enough.

There was also mistrust brewing, what would each person do with their money? Would they reinvest it in other businesses? Would they become independent and leave? Would people quit contributing their efforts in day-to-day operations?

Everyone has experiences they reflect on which are not pleasant. For me this is one of them. I felt pressure from our clients to lower our pricing, and employees wanting more pay, all of which was normal. But within our company we had a conflict with ownership and money. This became divisive and began to fracture our partnership.

When division comes it is very difficult to remove. Money and power are highly emotional things. Had we foreseen this challenge we could have invested more time in avoiding it. The reality was that division moved in like a 300 pound gorilla. The problem could not be avoided and managing it became an ongoing battle.

In the end there are times where there is no safe haven within business. It becomes you insulating and protecting yourself against your partners, employees, customers, vendors, everyone. There can be some very lonely times at the top of the mountain.

CHAPTER

PRESSURE

W hat does pressure feel like to you? What does it look like in a set of circumstances? What does it feel like internally? How do you react to pressure when it comes?

As a self proclaimed dreamer and one who tends to have a positive outlook on those dreams, I tend not to factor pressure in my dream time. There are no sharks in my blue water think tank.

Unfortunately sharks are a common occurrence in real blue water and if you are not expecting to encounter them when surrounded by raw meat, think again.

So my propensity for dreaming followed with strategic planning and then the execution didn't have contingencies for "what if things go wrong." I like to plan for things going right. The question is what to do when things end up not going as planned.

In late 1990's we had diversified our product range into more complex molded components, mostly nonstructural bodywork for motorcycles. We were now introducing new components.

Our real competitive advantage had been discovered. We knew this because we discovered the constraint within our clients organizations. They didn't have the ability to develop as many new products as they wanted as fast as they wanted. We offered this service for free or at low cost in exchange for production contracts.

An investment had been made in new manufacturing equipment and production areas were created. Men were trained in new techniques and controls were put in place. We began manufacturing many products for Yamaha and the first few years were a successful trial run.

In early 2001 we began working with Triumph Motorcycles, the same way we did with Yamaha, manufacturing their branded aftermarket components which were sold through their dealerships. The relationship gelled and we were asked to participate in manufacturing OEM components to come stock on the motorcycles right off the production line.

The contract was lucrative enough to augment the decline in sales from our core products. The exchange rate between the USA and England favored exportation of our products. I felt this business concept could be the pot of gold at the end of the rainbow which would fuel us into the next decade.

I spent time in the Triumph factory as their people did in ours. Triumph shipped motorcycles to us and we developed the components in our research and development area. New manufacturing processes were developed specifically for their uniquely designed components. Because that was the case, there were no text books. We were not worried though, small batch production had gone well, we were ready to launch.

Although there was a great reward, there was also a great risk. Triumph took OEM supply very seriously. If a supplier didn't deliver quality products on time, and the line was stopped due to your inept ability, your company would be charged a daily penalty equal to the profits lost from that production line. The loss amount could be staggering.

This was a calculated risk, one that needed to be taken because the decline of our core products was continuing, compounded by the fact we were headed toward the last four months of the year which always made our production line look like a ghost town.

I went through the mental check list: R&D? Done. Small batch manufacturing? Good. Equipment and production facilities? Ready. Twenty men hired and trained for two shifts? Check. All systems were in place and we were ready.

The deal was inked and we headed into production, I waited at the end of the rainbow for the pot of gold to be wire transferred into our account.

Unfortunately there were problems in paradise. Our first week yielded 50% waste, which was greater than our profit margin. There was a net loss. I met with our production managers and we went through the production logs, where was the problem?

I wanted to say, "lets kick this back to R&D and figure out where we went wrong," but that wasn't an option. We were bound by contract and BAX Global showed up every Friday to collect those 24" boxes and fly them across the Atlantic where, by Wednesday, they would be on a production line being fastened to a mechanical child in the making that was headed to a new home.

The weeks went by and I was now consumed with our production people solving a puzzle that seemed to be missing a few pieces. We never found them.

Production was ramped up to three shifts since waste remained high. Weeks rolled into months and we were losing money at $40,000 per month. The paper cut had turned into a bloody, gaping wound.

I could hear our competition squealing with glee. I could feel the weight of the anvils that my chest pumped up and down at 3 a.m. in a cold sweat. I could hear my mind screaming for a way out, day after day, as I had to exude confidence and quell fear in my production camp. I had to answer the hard questions, no bullshit, to my banker as they held me accountable. The equity was draining as I watched the needle move from F to E on our balance sheet. The pot of gold turned out to be a firing squad.

During this time I still had to be a loving husband and bring peace rather than turmoil into our home every evening. Four months earlier Janelle had given birth to our first born son. I was learning to be a dad and wasn't getting a lot of sleep. There were still commitments at my church to teach, give and participate in what we were doing. My brother was staying with us as he had just experienced personal tragedy in his life. There wasn't an area in my life I could let go of just because times were tough. There would be no excuses.

Although we did make solid improvements in the manufacturing process, lower the waste and slowed the bleeding, the bottom line was that we were saved by the misfortune of another. I received a panicked call one morning in my office from our buyer at Triumph. He explained there had been a massive fire the previous day, the factory had burnt to the ground like kindling next to a blowtorch. The governor had signed our stay of execution.

The negative cash flow had ended, the contract expired unfulfilled and we would live to fight another day. Some wins aren't pretty and this was one of them, but we were still alive, we had learned an incredible amount through high volume production on these types of components, which would later serve us well, when we would reunite with Triumph.

The pressure still remained, but it had morphed. I had been making difficult decisions in a tough environment for quite sometime. Now we were at the end of the fourth quarter, looking for core business to turn back up. I had to clean up the mess that was left behind and begin looking to the future. The bank was calling, employees were watching, my partners were questioning, I was thinking.

Sometime in December of 2001 I walked into our facility and laid off ½ of our production staff. We had no immediate workload to replace that which was lost from the fire at Triumph. Our cash flow was on life support. The fat hog had gone to slaughter.

There were other pot's forming at the end of our rainbow. Up ahead in the distance I could see them. A new niche market surfaced within our industry for the core products we had manufactured for so long. The business for molded components with Yamaha was expanding continually, and eventually Triumph would be back. We would streamline and keep that which was profitable, and cut the fat.

Through it all I learned something very intrinsic. Battles will come and go, they don't last forever and usually don't play out how we think they will. We may not be able to define what kind of battle we will face when entering a new endeavor in life, but we should know that there will be battles and we must accept the challenge of facing them. When in battle, it's important to keep your composure. Poor decisions are made usually under pressure.

Marriages are lost, children are alienated, careers are scrapped, dignity is shelved. Know that without winning the battle you can't win a war and enjoy the spoils of victory. Be careful what you wish for in becoming an entrepreneur, you might just get it all.

One of my favorite sayings is "don't brag like one who takes off his armor before you put it on". This wasn't the first battle I had faced, there had been many before and there would be more to come. I would be ready.

CHAPTER 25

REMOVE THE EMOTION

While dealing with the issues with Triumph, I began asking myself directional questions about where PCI was headed. More importantly how we would address the expansion of our molded component production line, we looked at the following as options:

1. **Borrow more money and hire additional qualified staff that can address the issue on a longer term basis.** Doing this within the USA would mean our margins could not support additional middle management. We would need to raise our prices to accommodate this, which would be difficult to do with pressure from China.

2. **Continue to move down the current path of problem solving with our current staff and find solutions within which would allow us to further grow.** I knew none of us had the skill set necessary to pull this off. It would be an uncertain road.

3. **Shut down the new production line, and lay off half our staff.** Downsize the company and focus solely on our core products.

4. **Move the company to Mexico** where we could build in more margin within the products to hire additional qualified middle management for new product development and production.

Over a very short period, and within a lot of pressure, we chose to pursue option three and four. We would close the production line, keeping our core products in production, rebuild our profitability and then move the company to Mexico.

So during the first week of November I walked into our facility and laid off about 20 people on the spot. I did it myself, I removed the emotion and I was very clear why we were shutting down that production line. The failure was both with management and with employees. I had decided that this was not in the best interest of the company. I let them go immediately.

Holding onto mediocre people to the detriment to the organization only leads to the destruction of the organization. With that in mind you must be a gate keeper and remove people who may have once been committed but now live in mediocrity. Unfortunately most of whom we let go were casualties of a failed expansion, but some managers had lost sight of the core principals we lived by.

I knew this was business, and good managers make the tough calls in difficult times and move on. There was no enjoyment in it, and ultimately I was the responsible party. I had to evaluate my own failures, and look for corrective measures before we tried again.

CHAPTER

THE TOUGH CALL

The truth was that were that our business was not big enough any longer to sustain three working partners drawing salaries and benefits, one of whom was not producing. I had shut down the production for OEM molded components and was looking to increase sales on core products while reducing overhead.

You may recall the information included earlier about the difference between a shareholder and an employee. Unfortunately that diluted state began to play out negatively within our organization.

Having an unproductive working partner consumed much of our available resource which could have been invested into new products, marketing, etc. In addition, people either make money or spend money. James was supposed to be managing tooling and fixtures for product development and production. He cost the company thousands of dollars monthly purchasing needless things which never produced for the organization.

Honestly he had good intentions but the pressure had become overwhelming. I brought in new contracts which needed components developed. Time and again he was unable to deliver the needed development to see the components into production.

We tried buying more sophisticated development equipment, better training programs, longer lead times, none worked. The pressure had infiltrated his heart and undermined his performance.

It became clear the company could not sustain the overhead long term. I consulted with Alex, we referenced the employment contract, and documented the failure over several months.

When the time was right we met as a team for the last time. I informed James that his services would no longer be needed. This did not affect his stock ownership, only his employment. It wasn't long after that he chose to liquidate through his buy/sell agreement and cashed out.

In the end we made the decision that was in the best interest of the organization by reducing overhead, and reallocating resource to more productive areas. It was a tough decision. There was a family behind the person, he had a wife and three children. It was tough for me because he was the last of the original partners and we had worked together for nearly ten years. The relationship would be over.

In the end James had to face the facts. Look at his own performance, his own contribution and see that it was not good enough in the current climate to remain on staff. Unfortunately he was unwilling to look at the circumstances objectively through the months leading up to his termination. An important lesson was penetrating my core.

We want to control employees, clients, suppliers, and markets, but allow ourselves to remain imperfect and uncontrolled. Why are we expecting everyone else to be perfect to offset our imperfection. Without finding and eliminating our own imperfections we will eventually be eliminated.

A very relevant investment of time is to set quarterly evaluations for myself. I did this for our company but it was important to set them for myself as well.

This included reflecting on the previous three months and seeing my shortfalls in leadership, cash flow management, decision making, systems modification, etc. A new set of issues to personally address would be developed. These are not goals but corrections I need to make. For me a list of three or four items to address is plenty.

I leave this on my Outlook to review weekly and press myself to make progress. At the end of the quarter I grade myself and see what progress the organization and I have made.

What I have learned is that I need a few things:

- I must be honest with myself about my performance
- I must set guideposts for personal development
- I must follow through to bring change
- I must have accountability from others concerning these changes

The truth is an important element in life. Without the truth we cannot correct our issues and continue to grow. Avoiding the truth may allow justification in your own eyes, however the world will not be so kind. Learn to honestly evaluate your performance and contribution. Remove the excuses.

CHAPTER 27

RESISTANCE

I have always enjoyed the process of evaluating stocks and charting fluctuations in stock value while looking at the factors that may have brought about the change. What interests me is that stocks assign a dollar value based on the perspective other humans have on that organization. Stocks quantify human organizations, or at least the perception of them.

There are so many factors that affect stocks. Obviously there are internal factors such as perspective from investors and external factors created by the market and overall economy. There is a vast framework underneath each of these three segments built like a web of countless decisions and actions all culminating in the stock value on the ticker tape.

Daily stock values are displayed on charts over a given span of time which reveal positive and negative fluctuations in the value. Stocks are not linear, they fluctuate continually. However stocks do have a range which they fluctuate within, rolling up and down over the course of time. When stocks are low they ultimately find "support" and when on the rise they meet "resistance". The fluctuations occur between support and resistance levels until something dramatic causes a positive or negative change and drives the stock to new higher or lower levels. People also float between support and resistance levels in their personal and professional lives. We just don't have a ticker tape to look at daily and see how we are doing.

The problem with being at the top of an organization is having nobody to hold you accountable on a daily basis. There is no boss looking over your shoulder pointing out mistakes and helping you correct them.

People at the top of an organization are responsible for finding their own deficiencies and correcting them. It's a grown-up scavenger hunt where if you find your issues and correct them, you win, but if you don't locate and eliminate deficiencies you lose. I believe this is one of the missing steps that keeps those who are successful in small business from progressing into being successful at the big business level.

The problem most successful small business owner's face is they never really hold themselves fully accountable for the success or failure of the organization. There is a certain amount of deception which everyone buys into. We all think we are better looking, smarter or more important than we really are. Nobody wants to be average! We must learn to ask ourselves, "what are my flaws and how do I change them?"

The support systems you have built in your life may insulate against some levels of failure but the invisible resistance is the killer of progress. This roll range between support and resistance in our lives represents our comfort zone. We reach that resistance in life where we need to change fundamental things about ourselves, which we may not even be aware of, and if we don't change we drift back down to our support level.

During that period of hitting resistance, I know I've become frustrated asking myself, "What am I doing wrong? Where are my flaws?" Some of which I didn't address until starting the next business venture. If we are going to grow and progress, we have to be brutally honest with ourselves. There must be a sobering self evaluation where core issues can surface. We must cut ties with the excuses we have held to like a security blanket. Once those are located, we must implement corrective measures that will cause us to break through the resistance we face. You must then create a framework for accountability to ensure long term results.

One of the biggest fundamental changes I incurred during leadership came when we moved our manufacturing to Mexico. I wanted a middle management team and I had a plan for creating one -- but could I lead and empower them? I would have to change my behavior before that would happen.

Collecting information for personal assessment can be challenging. We have to find ways to see ourselves through a perception other than our own.

This is obviously where partnerships can be more beneficial than being a sole owner of a business. Partnerships innately provide built-in accountability. This only works though if both partners are equally committed to being transparent about their shortcomings and both committed to helping each other become better.

If you can garner information from your employees, clients or

suppliers on the constraints they see in you and in your organization, you can get "real time" information much like a ticker tape.
Have you ever wondered why you haven't made the turn to
clear the hurdles you are facing? The answer lies with your own
inefficiencies. It's not the fault of your customers, suppliers, staff
or market. The state of your organization for better or worse is
a direct reflection of you. Your leadership, wisdom and management were good enough to get you to where you are, but not
good enough to get you beyond. This is why we must continue to
develop and move forward in personal development through assessment, implementation and accountability.

ASSESSMENT
Find ways of collecting information outside your
own perspective.

IMPLEMENTATION
Put a simple plan in place to bring personal change.

ACCOUNTABILITY
Share your faults and plan for change with someone who can
inquire about your progress.

28

FINDING THE TRUTH

Have you ever asked yourself "I wonder what really happened" after watching a documentary or reading a historical account of an event? Have you thought about the Kennedy assassination and wished you could find the truth? I am one of those guys who after watching a movie that was based on a true story, spends a week reading materials to dig deeper and see if I can find threads of truth that weave the real story.

When we initially moved our manufacturing operation to Mexico, there were many challenges through the process of ramping up production. I brought down our production manager to help influence the behavior and belief of the production workers as well as teach the skills necessary to produce our products.

Adding the middle management and removing me from day to day operations helped me overcome personal limitation of micro managing people. This was a transitional process for me because I couldn't depend solely on my problem solving abilities since manufacturing was now in Mexico. I had to teach others to problem solve, to help them connect with each other to resolve issues. I was becoming an identifier and mediator of issues. I was learning to bring clarity to issues, not just make decisions.

Belinda was our plant manager and had been managing this plant long before we moved our operation into it. She was in her forties, big glasses, big heart. She had obviously accomplished a lot to have gained the management position she had in a male dominated country. I liked her inquisitive nature and her "get it done" attitude.

To help oversee the operation from my office in the US, I implemented a series of four reports which were used to track core elements of the business. Regularly I would call Belinda and ask her a series of questions after reviewing the reports.

Our staff was new to the manufacturing processes and therefore the issues we faced seemed complex to them. We also had to change the culture of top down management style which was so evident in Mexico. These people were not used to problem solving issues and making judgment decisions. They were accustomed to reporting issues and waiting for management to decree the direction they must go.

In the beginning there were many trips to Mexico. More than I wanted, but it was part of the commitment necessary to making the program work as we ramped up. We were teaching people new skills and a new way to think. There wasn't anything easy about this process.

During one early trip to Mexico, Belinda and I were standing in the packaging area discussing business. She was talking with great passion about the current issues which needed addressing,

I was looking off in the distance, down part of the production line, watching men passing back and forth in their routines. How could we make this new complex process simple to evaluate. I said to her, "Belinda, all of the issues we face fall into two categories".

Failure of the system
OR
Failure of human resource to manage the system

"As plant manager your job is to find out which of the two failed, and either fix the system or correct the person."

We managed the plant with this one unique rule for problem solving. It was extremely effective because of the simplicity which makes the evaluation of issues crystal clear. Asking this question became the starting point for resolving issues. Each issue could be filtered through this lens to determine where the failure occurred. This made it easier to find a solution which would produce results, it didn't just salve a wound and mask fundamental flaws which could resurface.

If the failure was due to the system, we would modify it to keep the issue from reoccurring. If the failure was due to a mistake by human resource, we could respond with better training, accountability or disciplinary measures. Every failure we encountered we first asked, "What failed: the system or the people?"

The psychology of this process filtered through our organization because we promoted people of discipline who could effectively manage the systems we had in place as well as resolve flaws within the systems. The more effectively people managed the systems, the more accurate reading we could get as to whether the system was functioning correctly and then determine our next steps.

Belinda gained much confidence from this method. It helped to reduce the vastness of a new manufacturing process to isolating individual issues and finally determining the root cause. Finding the truth is how we get better. Sometimes we just need a simple way to discover it.

CHAPTER

NUMBERS DON'T LIE

Nearly all accomplishments or failures in life can be boiled down to numbers. Scholars are measured by their grades. Athletes are ranked by their statistics. Politicians are promoted by votes.

Businesses are graded by their financial statements.

Numbers, accurate real numbers always tell the truth. Numbers do not care about circumstance or the battlefields traversed to produce them. They don't care how many late nights you studied for school, how many injuries you overcame in athletics, the number of speeches given to win votes, how many risks you took to build your business. Numbers measure the results after a series of decisions and actions. Numeric measurement is the scorecard to all production in life. They force you to leave the excuses at the door.

I love numbers, which is strange to me. I don't see myself as a numbers guy, but I am a truth guy so by default I am a numbers guy. Don't tell me the war stories, just show me the numbers!

Overseeing manufacturing in Mexico from an office in Tulsa had limitations. I couldn't walk down to the production floor when there was an issue and see it for myself. I had to find new ways to gather real information, not just listen to stories.

There were plenty of stories that came from our facility by e mail and telephone. Understandably, there was a familiarization process from the staff to our way of doing things. There was some insecurity within them due to the unknown. Every issue had layers which needed to be peeled back like an onion.

Everyone who has managed people has dealt with pride: self preservation over unveiling the truth. Diluted information leads to bad decisions.

I was convinced that with the right information, manufacturing could be managed from the north side of the Mexican border. What was the right information? There were four components that went into information gathering:

- **Accurate information**
- **Real time information**
- **Simple information**
- **Complete information**

ACCURATE INFORMATION

The accuracy of the information was completely dependant on our people being disciplined to record unbiased data. Numbers could not be manipulated to derive a certain perspective. This was like an unforgivable sin which meant immediate dismissal. At the end of the day, you have to trust those who are collecting data.

REAL TIME INFORMATION

Real time information is critical in finding and solving problems before they cause real damage. However it can be difficult to get real time information from production workers within your organization. Most workers see little value in gathering and recording information because it doesn't add to their productivity, it actually reduces it. I had to stress to my employees that it contributed to our productivity as managers. Information was critical to Belinda, the engineers and myself to make good decisions. Placing equal value on the prompt reporting of information stimulated the reporting process on the production floor. We often rewarded the accuracy and on time delivery of reports.

The reports also had to be easily recorded. We didn't want managers walking around collecting data all day, the workers could do that. We just made it easy on them. Clipboards were placed in various locations throughout the facility for workers to record specific information, which was then put into spreadsheets and formatted for easy mental digestion.

SIMPLE INFORMATION

Simplicity of information is critical. What you attempt to measure must be clearly defined. For instance, I wanted to understand the time that was spent in each phase of the manufacturing process. This was critical because we ran three shifts nonstop. If one shift did not complete their work on time, it meant the next shift could not complete their work load. Since you can't create time, if one shift ran late, the next shift had to drop production.

The downward spiral was a difficult master. The first shift spent too many labor hours producing components, driving cost up, while the second shift was unable to complete their work, which translates to more cost per part produced.

Typically there would be stories and ramblings of why the production was not completed on time. We wanted to measure exactly where in the production cycle time was lost rather than depending on human perspective.

The production process included about ten phases. We measured the time elapsed at each phase and set an acceptable baseline. When parts were being processed the lead man would record the time elapsed for each phase. If production fell behind we could review this sheet and find exactly which phase was causing issues, and investigate what caused the delay. Now the numbers were in black and white and we could find the area where the problem existed. To find a problem easily you must have simple, accurate information. Remember that you can never solve a problem until it is defined.

COMPLETE INFORMATION

Having complete information is critical because if you overlook a single area, you could have missed an area where failure is causing a leak in your money boat. It is impossible to know all of the items to monitor with a start up operation. The key is being vigilant to review your business model and continue discovering those areas which need numeric supervision.

As you find issues, resolve them through the implementation of a modified system, make sure you also implement a monitoring system. Accountability is the key to making sure that people are operating systems as they are designed. Reporting systems ensure that operational systems are being executed and sustained. Let me provide a few examples:

PRODUCTION

Are we making the parts for the cost we thought we could and to the quality specified?

SALES

Do we know what the minimum number of sales are that we need on a weekly basis? What are the steps required to generate those sales? Cold calls, sales calls, estimating, etc.

PRODUCT TRENDS

Do we see the subtle changes in market demand for our products and how those affect future product design?

MARKETING

Do we track specific marketing plans and their effectiveness? Why would we continue spending money on marketing that does not work?

OVERHEAD

How much should overhead cost for what we are producing and how do we measure up to that guidepost?

PROFITABILITY

Do we properly understand and track all the phases which contribute to real profitability and how do we know it's accurate? Positive cash flow is the life blood of any business. If you slit your wrists how long can you survive?

Every business is different and it's impossible to create any sort of master list that all businesses use. I would prefer to leave you with a thought process rather than a how-to manual. You need to be as vigilant at collecting and evaluating statistical information as you are any other phase of your business.

Cindy, my accountant, is known as the principal. Going to her office to review financials has always reminded me of sitting behind the desk of my grade school teachers, ready to hear the outcome of my report card before taking it home to my parents.

As the president or CEO of any organization knows, quarterly financial statements are your report card, reflecting the performance of your organization. How we quantify each phase of our business down to numerical values often determines how well we identify tangible progress or failure. Hopefully this information can help you make beneficial decisions in real time which will result in all A's on the next report card from your accountant.

CHAPTER

SUSTAINING MOMENTUM

Saturday was chore day around our house. I regularly bucked the system in an attempt to avoid any manual labor. I was still required to do my fair share no matter the attitude I had.

There were chores like shoveling snow, splitting and carrying fire wood in the winter. Spring and summer meant mowing the lawn and cleaning the garage. Everyday was a day with dirty dishes. I remember when my mom showed me how to iron my own dress shirts for church when I was about 12. Today I still think I am better at ironing than my wife.

When I started working for money as a young teenager I didn't mind nearly as much cutting grass or shoveling snow because I had purpose, I wanted money. We have that same drive and ambition when we first start our businesses, and that is usually very attractive to those new clients. Smart buyers always look for "hungry" companies to do business with.

Over time attitudes can change and people become jaded to

the small details. Issues that arise become irritations to be avoided rather then new battles which lead to new green pastures.

I think one of the biggest mistakes I made in business was allowing myself to believe that I had graduated or grown beyond having to do certain fundamental activities or address difficult issues head on.

Pride is deceptive and it creeps in like carbon dioxide. It's an invisible gas which is virtually undetectable but eventually it will lull you into unconsciousness. People can insulate themselves from problem areas within their business. Not addressing them can allow this cancer to spread and infect healthy areas of your business. Ignoring problems will not make them go away.

What I am referring to is your willingness to be involved in areas that you do not like or have little interest in. We can never insulate ourselves completely from being involved in activities that we do not like. An attempt to develop and insulate for comfort is counter productive to advancement and productivity.

Are you willing to do whatever it takes to be successful? If you lose that edge, then you have left your business vulnerable and open for attack from your competition who may have that drive to go beyond your current level of comfort. Do you remember how hungry you were when you started out? That is how you have to be today. If you are just starting please know you will never arrive at a place where that internal willingness and humility is not needed. Any such arrival for a business is greeted with an open casket from your competition.

Mature businesses always leave open doors of vulnerability. Start up businesses are successful because they recognize and find a way to exploit that open door. When an attack is launched against a vulnerable business, that organization must address the willingness of it's people to change before the external issues can be changed.

Your mindset must be a willingness to do the task that is required at the time to move your organization forward no matter what it is. That mindset must be filtered throughout your human resource but it starts with you. Your company will start failing when you are no longer willing to do whatever it takes. If you find yourself in this position you only have two choices:

> **1. Change your level of commitment.**
> **2. Get out of the business.**

We have to make our decisions based on productivity rather than comfort. It comes back to doing what is in the best interest of the company, and you are not exempt from the golden rule.

I routinely ask myself, what am I unwilling to do now that I was willing to do when I started? Have I provided sufficient personnel in that area to cover that block of work? If I left holes I need to develop a solution. I must always be willing to contribute where and when I am needed.

When we moved our plant to Mexico we located our American production manager at the facility to train the new staff. It was a highly stressful position and one that required incredible commitment on his part. Unfortunately after a few weeks he headed to Vegas for a long weekend and never returned.

I was the qualified person to train people on all systems and positions, so I headed off to Mexico during the holidays for an extended stay. Even though I didn't want to do it, I did what was in the best interest of the company and that was to get the new facility production efficient.

CHAPTER 31

COLLATERAL DAMAGE

When a country goes to war one of the most difficult items to address is collateral damage. A decision must be made up front as to the amount and type of collateral damage that will be accepted in exchange for the potential gains. Loss of life and resource is a guarantee in war - but to what extent?

After I left PCI and was pursuing other endeavors. I found myself in Taiwan enjoying a dinner with three successful businessmen. One of the three I had a particular affinity toward because early on in his career he had raced cars professionally.

We talked of business, Asian politics and many other topics. At one point in the meal he was describing some of the elements he had come in contact with in China's interior. "There are many dark corners in China" he commented. I thought for a long time about this statement and I think it fits into entrepreneurship as well.

There are also many dark corners in business. Being naive of their existence and not considering their impact can cause you to make decisions that have a high price attached to them.

People don't see the collateral damage they can have in their lives or cause in other's lives through poor decision making in business. When you are single and in your early twenties it's difficult to measure or even consider the impact that a particular business model, market, partnership or lifestyle can have on your future. How business can affect your marriage, children, friends, even your psychology and perspective on life, is grossly underestimated.

Decisions cannot be made solely on gains in profitability. Consideration must be given to the people who will be effected directly and indirectly by the decision.

I see people who lose their marriages, health, happiness and children over business. They love business so much they are willing to risk and lose everything for greater success. Please understand that success does equate to happiness or satisfaction. The means will never justify the end. Choose to set non-negotiable boundaries that your decisions are filtered through. Your success should enhance your life rather than being your life.

32

PASSION VS COMMITMENT

So many people preach "passion" in business today. Hire passionate people. Promote passionate people. Be passionate people! I disagree. Passion is an emotion, and we should all know by now that emotions change -- and change frequently. Circumstances internally and externally effect our emotions positively as well as negatively.

So what happens when you hire a person to manage your accounts and six months into the position your largest three clients leave the company? Your new sales manager is now faced with a mighty big challenge in the midst of high pressure. His emotion of excitement might not be the same. You can expect he might come in and say that he is no longer "passionate" about what he is doing.

Passion fades...

If we are not hiring passion, what should we hire? Hire commitment! What we want are people who are committed. Commitment supersedes passion, commitment doesn't change with emotions. Commitment is a decision, not an emotion. People who are committed can rise above their emotions and navigate difficult situations, because they are driven to achieve an end goal.

What do committed people look like? I recently had a young intern who played four years of college football and never got into a single game until his final one. His commitment to the team superseded his passion for playing football. I would rather hire him than the star quarterback.

When we moved our manufacturing facility from San Louis to Tecate, Mexico I had to make a decision about who would be the plant production manager. At our first facility we had several engineers on staff. We had a woman with about 15 years of experience who was an effective manager. We also had two engineers, one who aspired to be the plant manager and the other who aspired to do a great job. His name was Noe, and was in his late twenties.

I had noticed during our first year of working together that he had a propensity to learn and do better. When moving the plant to Mexico initially Noe was involved in problem solving all the production issues and assisting in setting up the production lines.

One day Noe and I went out to Taco Chello to get some lunch. We drove the back streets of San Luis in his early 90's Impala. Taco Chello was a favorite lunch spot for much of our management team. It was on the corner of a quiet street, a humble building probably only seating about 20 people. The walls were oak, with simple décor. There was a grill and cash register at one end, benches resembling church pews were stuffed into the floor space.

Nobody spoke English which left me dependant on Noe for ordering. We always got the same things, five tacos each, served on a wooden plate with a handle, and of course a coke to wash it down.

As we drove toward Taco Chello I asked Noe how he had learned to speak English. He told me he taught himself by watching cartoons in English when he was a child. This spoke volumes about his internal commitment to accomplishing goals and from that I knew he would make a great plant manager.

His commitment surfaced as we faced challenges with personnel, systems and processes. The senior engineer and the plant manager were more concerned with the politics and jockeying for position. Noe had his head down and was committed to getting the company to reach the outlined goals.

When the plant went on strike it was Noe's house that I visited on Sunday, in a plea to discuss with him what was in the best interest of the company, and therefore its people. He understood this concept and regardless of great pressure was willing to look at the situation objectively. He was committed to resolving the situation.

When we moved the plant to Tecate I used Noe to help hire and train the staff. He orchestrated the leadership and transfer of many workers who came with us. Initially Noe did not carry the title but he was the plant manager. I knew I could call him at 2 a.m. and we could discuss an issue because he slept with his phone.

His commitment overrode many emotions and situations. I chose the man with the least experience, but the highest commitment. I believe it paid off. His experience level increased rapidly because his commitment and pliability kept him in a position to learn.

All businesses face difficult challenges, the worst of which come when an organization is in negative cash flow. Difficult periods last as long as it takes the management to find the problem and implement solutions that bring positive change. However, it must be executed in a highly emotional environment where extreme pressure may be present.

People that can operate within those difficult environments are required to get through difficult challenges. People equipped to work well under stress dramatically shorten the time an organization spends in difficult environments. If you surround yourself with people who are passionate, they will run for cover when the heat comes, if you find people who are committed, the heat isn't so bad.

33

THIS ISN'T BUSINESS (BUT IT IS)

J ames was now gone, the volume production line for Triumph shut down, and we were regrouping to take another run. We spent a year making ourselves financially whole again and began to find new markets for our core products, which were very promising. But pressure was coming in from China with low cost manufacturing and I knew it would drive our prices and margins down. The new upward swing in volume for our core products would be offset by the lower margins and the net gain for the company would be minimal.

If we were going to expand the company in the future we had to find a way to get middle management employed, and do that without disturbing the monthly overhead. I began searching for ways to move our facility to Mexico which would reduce our cost basis in each part and make room to hire some middle management which would give us the human resource to explore new products and processes.

It took about a year for me to find a suitable partner and the relationship seemed to fit like a glove. I had located a company which produced composite archery arrows whose business had constricted heavily from overseas pressure. We faced similar issues from the market.

They had a fantastic facility but an excess of employees. The manufacturing process was similar to ours, so I knew the people could adapt to our production methods. We signed a contract with their Maquila Dora (Mexican corporation) to produce products for us, but under a unique set of circumstances.

The agreement was structured to give us control of day to day management. We had our own staff, that were employees from the arrow manufacturing line who transferred to our side of the facility. We took over ½ the floor space and approximately ½ the people but we shared the plant manager.

We paid a per piece price to their corporation, but the price was fixed annually under a five year deal. We allowed for varying costs in materials and supplies, but fixed their profit margins. I finally had what I wanted:

- **A fixed price for the product**
- **Control over production scheduling**
- **Profit margin to put middle management in place**

It was incredible. Really I am extremely proud of the concept and how it was executed. Pro Sports got a volume contract for production to keep the maquila employees busy which was their objective. Both companies were happy with the outcome.

The relationship started out very strong. I spent the 2004 holiday season in Mexico at the plant training staff, implementing systems and ramping up production. Within 120 days we had sold our facility in Tulsa and I was in an office building downtown, managing sales, production and product development.

We had our two engineers, quality control team, inventory control and plant manager. I had a middle management team who were very capable. By our fourth month of production we eclipsed our best month ever logged in the USA over a 12 year period. We beat the mark by nearly 20%. I had more time and more money to develop new markets, and was very content that the plan was working. I felt vindicated.

But as the year wore on there were ripples in the water which represented an upcoming storm for which I was unprepared. Pro Sports had received a substantial shipment of materials from our sole supplier. It was their responsibility to procure the materials and pay for them. Since the contract was established with them, in essence as a subcontractor, we were now a third party in the transaction with no direct responsibility.

Our materials had to remain frozen because heat caused the chemicals to react and therefore spoil. The shipping company delivered a refrigerated load of materials to Mexico which was stored in a walk-in freezer. Something went wrong along the way and the chemicals expired before the material could be used in production. A dispute arose over whose responsibility it was between Pro Sports, the trucking company and the materials manufacturer.

Nobody wanted to take responsibility in the issue and a

$100,000 bill remained unresolved. Production ground to a halt
as raw materials in inventory were used up. I attempted to negotiate an agreement; however none of the parties were willing to
concede. We faced a major crisis because production was being
impeded.

I was sitting at my desk on the 11th floor of the downtown
building where we rented floor space. I always wondered what it
would be like to work inside one of them. Clean and pristine was
my image of business. No dirt under the nails of those guys. The
phone rang and I was about to find where they hid the dirty work.

It was a call from the owner of Pro Sports, he was going bankrupt. His arrow contracts had all but dried up and the portion of
the overhead which he held could not be financed on our business
alone. Our business model was contingent of him maintaining
his arrow business, of which we had no control over or knowledge.

Within two weeks we were closing down. I immediately had to
decide whether or not to purchase the arrow business and try to
make a go of that, along with ours. After evaluating his numbers,
there was nothing to buy.

Another choice was to take over the facility and employees
completely. We would have to attempt to cash flow the overhead,
which wasn't possible financially, without increasing our production volumes or borrowing more money.

We could move the facility back to the States and run a shell
of a company. I might have scratched out a salary but with price
pressures from China, there wasn't much meat left on the bone. I
didn't like losing the opportunity of future growth.

The final choice was to move our equipment from the facility,
start our own Maquila Dora, hire our people at a new location and
begin in Mexico again. The loss of production would shut our

doors for nearly two months.

Those few months were probably the most difficult time I had experienced in business. There was a flurry of activity in a very short period of time from many different fronts. Here is a short list of issues I faced simultaneously:

- **I had to explain to our bank the current state of events**; our subcontractor was going bankrupt and production has stopped.
- **I had to convince them to still loan us money** to open another facility.
- **I had to communicate with our clients that our production was halted for a short period of time**, and help them navigate delivery delays, while communicating confidence that we would be back in production shortly. A full disclosure of the main issues was discussed. We faced a real possibility of losing clients to overseas competition during our transition.
- **I had to convince our materials supplier to sell us materials directly**, as their $100,000 bill was still being disputed from Pro Sports, who was soon to be bankrupt.
- **I had to convince our current, trained core management and employees to wait for the new plant to open and transition their employment.**
- **I had to file for the Maquila, get a facility and build out completed, and move our equipment.**

My life was about preserving the supply chain, internal management structure, and distribution network. Remember, without compression spark and fuel, no engine can run. We were in jeopardy of losing one of our components and therefore destroying the cash flowing business.

In and of itself, the above list would be challenging to execute, but we hit another hurdle. I received another phone call.

We were enjoying a few minutes of peace on a Friday evening as we celebrated my second son's birthday. The phone call was from Belinda, our plant manager. She was extremely emotional as she attempted to communicate the following details.

The owner of Pro Sports was bringing trucks to the facility on Sunday to move out all of his equipment, ours would be left behind. This didn't seem bad until she explained Mexican law. Because Mexico is a socialist government, during bankruptcy or a plant strike, the government can seize the equipment within the building and sell it to compensate the employees for wages or severance packages due.

Any Mexican employee was due a severance package, which escalated in value with each passing year. Some of these employees had been with the company for over 10 years and the compensation would be high multiplied by dozens of workers.

He was attempting to remove his equipment and leave ours behind, which would cause my equipment to be impounded and liquidated by the government to cover the back taxes and wages due his employees. He knew that when the employees showed up on Monday and the majority of the equipment was gone, they would strike. This would lock up the facility causing a very negative set of events for my company. This was the first time I encountered bad business ethics in a time of trouble. It wouldn't be the last.

I was appreciative Belinda informed me of this move. He had not informed his employees or our company of his move, but my relationship with Belinda proved to be strong. Her loyalty was now with us. Alex flew to Mexico within a few hours and I arrived the next day. We hired a trucking firm to remove our equipment, hopefully on Saturday night, with the help of Belinda, but the employees got wind and filed a strike, locking down all of our equipment and Pro Sports as well.

Sunday morning I was, once again, driving the back streets of San Luis looking for the home of one of our engineers. I had hoped to negotiate the strike through him.

We also filed court papers, after a $40,000 deposit to a local attorney, who assured he could get our equipment back within a few weeks. Without the equipment released in a hurry, we would miss our delivery dates to our clients. Their contracts would be canceled and our distribution would end. Another call to the bank, more money wired in hopes of a resolution.

Fortunately within two weeks our equipment was released. A judge issued a court order which allowed us to cross the picket line, load up and leave. It took the Federales and guns to get us through a very hostile environment. We were about $100,000 poorer, another two weeks behind, but relieved nonetheless. We were headed to Tecate, Mexico to open our second plant and start again.

Interestingly enough the truth always surfaces in matters like this. I was prepared to hire and train a new staff from scratch, but our core employees learned the truth and many called to ask if they could join the team again. I was happy to receive them. We helped them relocate to Tecate during the facility build out and prepared for production.

I began to focus again on rebuilding the supply chain since the internal management was coming together and our customers were still committed. One last component and the engine would be running again.

After a decade of good business, our materials supplier was uninterested in selling us materials unless we cleared the $100,000 debt left by our subcontractor, and it had to be paid up front. Although we did not owe the debt, they were unwilling to take another risk on supply. The bank was not interested in loaning more money and I we were not interested in leveraging additional funds. We had to find another supplier.

Our products required very specific materials. It was not easy locating another supplier, but we did. Out on the east coast a small materials supplier had what we needed. I placed an order and sent a deposit check and we sat back for 30 days waiting for the refer truck to bring our goods.

Time was critical, the facility was nearly complete and the employees would be ready to start production. My wife and I were at lunch sitting outside a quaint restaurant. I called our new supplier a week prior to the ship date just to make sure we were still on schedule. Nobody had any answers on our order. I moved up the food chain until I reached the president who informed me they bumped our order for 30 days while they produced an order for their largest client. My emotions ran over at this restaurant as I lost control. They had the deposit, we had been scheduled for production and given a ship date, not even a phone call to alert us there was a problem. I demanded a refund and flew out to pick up the check personally.

While on the east coast I visited additional suppliers. Through a chain of events found a materials supplier who had what we needed in stock. The material quality was not as good, and our waste would be higher but it would get cash flowing and allow us to deliver product again.

Two weeks later I was in Tecate, helping to ramp up production again. Over the next two months I came home two weekends per month. It was the holidays I was lonely, tired, physically sick with pneumonia, but working hard to ramp up the production process, and service our customers.

Our customers had waited patiently, but the door had been opened. Our largest customer was now dual sourcing and the other supplier was from China. I knew it wouldn't be long before that supplier discovered our other customers too.

During this period I felt as if my partner had completely abandoned me. He was working hard building his other business while still collecting his paycheck from our company. He was convinced we wouldn't make it and fear was creeping in. I was most certainly carrying the burden for this transition and the survival of our business and my livelihood. Division was at the door of our partnership.

Entrepreneurs usually count on things going right. If I am guilty of anything it is that I plan for things to work out. I didn't plan on any of these events taking place. This was not what I envisioned business to be like, but the reality was that this was business. I could not foresee these situations nor did I expect them but when they occurred I had to navigate them whether I wanted to or not.

Sometimes business isn't what we envisioned it would be; but it's still business.

LEADERSHIP — IT IS WHAT IT IS

I feel bloated from consuming the free flow of information on leadership. I have purposefully restrained from heavy dialogue on this topic, but no business journey is taken without leadership being a major contributing factor. Therefore I must throw in my two cents to the federal reserve of leadership discussion.

The journey of leadership in business has three components:

> 1. What type of person is following you?
> 2. How have you defined the destination?
> 3. What can you lead your people through?

Who you have the ability to lead is the most critical component in an organization's success. The quality, strength, character and commitment level your people have will inevitably determine the strength and scope of your organization. It's greater than your market sector, product, systems, marketing strategy and any other ingredient within business. Why? Because the quality of person you have will determine how well your organization navigates the unknown situations you will face.

In my early years I attracted my buddies who wanted a place to work when they got out of college. I attracted people of similar interests and hobbies. It didn't take long to realize that difficult situations could not be navigated on the bond of recreation and good times. Turnover was fairly routine our first few years. It wasn't until I learned the value of leadership that I started connecting the dots.

In retrospect the transformation that I went through was unique for me in that I had to confront some harsh realities. The destinations were clearly defined in my heart, and I have always carried very deep convictions personally and professionally. Revealing those to a point of vulnerability and communicating them with confidence was my challenge. I never enjoyed being vulnerable about what I could see and how I saw us getting there.

Defining where we were going meant I had to lay down some armor with our employees and potentially take some shots professionally. Through a natural growing process I became vulnerable enough to communicate what I could see internally, and through hearing myself communicate that vision, I gained confidence.

The type of people who followed me changed once I verbalized my destination and realized the route necessary to get there. The transitional process was difficult because many thought this was just a ruse. They didn't feel that it was the authentic "me" because they had known a different me in the past. The professional and personal "me" were two separate characters. As I changed it demanded those around me to change too. Those who were unwilling were jettisoned from our organization in exchange for people who were attracted to our vision.

The vision and the communication of that vision became a source of strength for me. The fluctuations in personal relationship became less relevant. I began connecting with people because of a common vision instead of similar hobbies. I was taking our company to a specific destination. I was confident we could get there. People who wanted to be a part of that were magnetized, those who didn't weren't necessarily repelled -- but they didn't stick. Our staff may not have had a commonality of outside interests but it did hold a commonality of vision and drive.

The depth of that unity determines where and how far we would can go and ultimately determine what we would make it though. I had to lead employees through some difficult times. We had market challenges from China, cash flow crunches, fluctuation in market demand for our product, and our relocation process to Mexico.

How well the destination is defined and mapped out ultimately determined the people who were attracted to our organization. The strength, commitment and unity of those people determined how well we navigated battles we went through.

Unfortunately it also contributed to our unwinding. My vision for business became a mistress. When I sold a portion of my shares in PCI, I began investing in another business that I had been in the process of starting. I had fulfilled what I wanted to accomplish at PCI and therefore could not define the next new destination within the company. People saw my interests were divided and the destination became unclear for PCI. Their commitment faded. Quality people left and I was uninterested in finding, training and leading new people for an old organization.

As I reflect on this business venture, I come to two personal realizations. Although, I gained an understanding of the components that make up the leadership journey I did not master them. Having an understanding of leadership does not make me a great leader. I was a moderate, developing leader. The leadership ended when my commitment ended and that splintered the organization from the inside out. Everything in a company can be delegated except for leadership. If you are not committed to leading, don't worry, it won't take long for there to be nothing left to lead.

CHAPTER 35

MY BIGGEST MISTAKE

There are many components determining the "value" of a product. Things like price, quality, and service. The biggest difference between local and national companies is the difference in where they put the emphasis of "value." All companies have a mixture of the above qualities to arrive at "value" the difference is how people mix the components to achieve it.

Most local stores depend on relationship as the key ingredient: the owner becomes the brand. Alternately, national chains build brand image.

I know of a local coffee shop close to a local university campus. It's cool, trendy, hip and all the other conundrums a good coffee shop should be. However, its core focus is the owner. People feel like they know him and so they continually go back. People go to Starbucks because they know the white cup with the green logo and brown sleeve. Customers make the connection.

During our first run, in my twenties, I loved being "the man". I took great pride in finding the answer to difficult questions, doing what I felt was the "important work". I valued my contribution above others and I was untrusting of delegating high responsibility to others.

This meant I had the key relationships with suppliers and with customers. It also meant that if there was a major problem in production, I was the answer man. The only answer man.

Over time this created a culture where people were reluctant to take responsibility. This eventually created a two fold trap for the company:

1. **A culture had been created where real advancement had to come through me.**
2. **When I became disinterested in having all important decisions come through my office it was nearly impossible to change the mindset of the employees to want to accept responsibility.**

I built PCI to run through my office rather than building it to run independently of my office. Ultimately you want to be a contributor (but not mandatory) to the success of your organization.

Creating an organization with this type of culture allows for unlimited expansion. But to achieve this you must empower others to make decisions, and build a framework for their decision making process. You must become a teacher a coach, a builder of structure. Others then build the organization around you, but not through your office.

As your core people lean these traits, it allows the organization to continue breeding underneath them, which is their opportunity for advancement.   There is a sense of freedom for all involved. Any one person can leave and the culture can sustain the company and it now becomes a salable entity rather than a slave driver.

This transition was difficult for me. I worked hard to develop this structure when we moved the manufacturing operations to Mexico but I was far from perfecting it.

Are you the only connection for your business?
This system is dangerous for several reasons.

- You become the constraint and the organization cannot expand as it needs to.
- There is limited opportunity for others to grow.
- You cannot step away without the business suffering, which makes you a slave to the organization.
- The business is not a saleable entity allowing your departure.

CHAPTER 36

LETTING GO OF THE ROPE

Have you ever been waterskiing? I loved water skiing growing up. Of all those days skiing one memory has always stuck with me. One day in March my dad and I went to our little lake house. It was freezing cold - probably in the 50's. I felt a need to go skiing. We pulled the boat out of the slip and I sat off the end of the dock, legs dangling about 12 inches above the water sitting in my aqua and pink Jams. All of a sudden my dad pulled me off the dock and I was skiing on the glass like water.

I skied for a while and we headed toward a beach where I had planned to ski up onto the sand standing up, never going under water. Just as in business plans rarely ever go to script. As we neared the beach my dad cut the motor which created slack in the rope. I felt my legs start to sink as I frantically raised the rope above my head to try and take out the slack but it wasn't enough.

My dad noticed I was going down like a sack of potatoes and

immediately gunned the engine. The slack disappeared from the rope and my arms jerked downward. My legs were straight as I was trying to stay above the water's surface and the momentum pulled me forward which sent me sliding across the water. As the moment went from bad to worse I was submerged underwater, arms pumped and burning, holding my breath. Finally, I let go of the rope.

It was early December but being in San Diego you'd never know it. I was in a long-sleeved dress shirt and jeans, boarding an American Airlines flight to come home. It was nearly Christmas and I'd been in Mexico again for a few weeks. It had been a challenging trip. We were in production but running high waste, which was crippling our cash flow. It was clear we were feeling the effects of losing our original supplier.

There were promising signs that the resolution was near. An early formulation for resin was relocated and I was certain we could re-implement the old formula and regain our composure.

I had been away from home far too much. My wife and kids felt distant for the first time ever. It was like they were a separate family and I was visiting them. One of the most valuable things in my life has always been coming home from the office and getting mobbed by my kids as I walked through the door. Now I was concerned they were developing a life without me.

I took my window seat in first class and slipped my computer bag underneath the seat in front of me. No longer did I travel reading the latest "get to the next level" book.. In the past I would have fought for the isle seat during the reservations process. It all seemed so petty now. I was wasted tired.

We went through the usual drama and were shortly in the air heading to DFW. I gazed out the window at the scenery as we were served a cold beverage as if all the people in first class had somehow crossed the desert and were in need of emergency medical treatment.

When I first started flying I used to love to talk to the other passengers. In my 20's it was all so new and exciting. I was interested in what everyone was up to and could even learn something from the back side of the barf bag. Now I wasn't even interested in myself. But for some reason I muttered the word "hello" and forced a smile toward the man sitting next to me.

He responded with small talk. Somehow we went through the normal pecking order of sniffing each other like dogs to determine who had the more prestigious position, who made more money, who flew more miles. Yada yada yada.

During the small talk he said something I had heard recently from several others. Regardless of his line of work his comment boiled down to his son graduating from high school. The business man was upset that he had missed his son's childhood – all because of work.

"But you know there is nothing you can do about it," he said. Like it was a badge of honor to give up your family, marriage, kids, for business. For money. But I heard it all the time while flying -- men proud of the fact they played the harlot. Always describing being away for their companies, careers, etc.

"I know it's tough but you don't have any other choice," said a purchasing agent to me just the week prior.

"But I had no choice," said another friend of his failed relationship with his son.

In one brief moment I processed the events of the past few years, the market, the partnership, the plant in Mexico and realized that I was in complete control of my circumstances. I was in control and I did have a choice. I could choose to do something else if I wanted to.

Because it was year end our accountant began auditing the books. We found some major irregularities in my partner's book-keeping. The details are irrelevant but the actions were unethical and potentially illegal. When I confronted my partner about the issues at hand, he was unwilling to correct them, returning the money and property which was missing.

When I compiled all of the details in my mind, I knew that a business would never stand where the partners could not trust each other. It was time for me to make a choice, to let go of the rope.

I took all the information to my banker and asked him to call our notes due and foreclose on the business so that the bank and myself could avoid any additional damage. The next six months were very difficult as we unwound the business and liquidated assets. It was not the kind of environment that I enjoy. In the end I chose not to sue him for damages. Those situations are messy and take years to resolve. There is usually heavy time, monetary and emotional investment to prove you were right and collect the money due you. There were two questions I asked myself:

1. **Was I right?** Yes, I knew I was right, the facts were very cut and dry. My perspective was that he was scared and trying to grab some gold since Rome was burning.

2. **Was suing him going to be the easiest way to protect my investment?** No. Suing him was a long arduous process and one I was not interested in pursuing. For me it was just easier to go and start another business and make money the old fashioned way, earn it.

Let me comment here about my partner. I don't think he was a bad person. I often think about the Germans or Japanese during World War II. They were considered the "bad guys" but when the war ended we hired the smartest Nazi's to work on our space program and they became the "good guys". In other words sometimes the line is blurred on who the good and bad guys really are. I think he just made some poor decisions.

In writing this book it would be easy for me to paint him as the bad guy and that isn't my intent. He made some decisions with poor judgment. But I also understand he was scared, and didn't think we would make it. He had invested a lot of money and was frustrated things did not go as planned. I can see why he made the decision he did, although they were unethical. Taken in context over the six years we were in business together this instance was somewhat out of character for him. My disappointment was that we could not find a resolution. Performance Composites submerged us in the icy waters of business.

I finally let go of the rope.

CHAPTER

THE FOUNDATIONAL CONTRACT

As it stands there is one contract that has brought me great strength and security throughout my business career. It has been the underlying current of support throughout my adult life. The strength of the contract has overridden the emotions of insecurity, fear and weakness at times when I have experienced through the adventure of business.

Although the contract was drafted for others, I was fortunate enough to be grafted into the contract by adoption, which happens to be a last will and testament including a trust fund. I've seen some pretty complex trusts in my time but this one takes the cake.

My adoption was complete around the age of 13 but I had no

understanding of the trust, the provisions and the responsibilities that came along with it until my late twenties. Since then it's been an adventure of discovery and an embracement through understanding of the responsibility to my family.

The understanding really began in my early twenties as I began to spend time with the attorney who is the executor of the trust. He has always been faithful to meet me in the most inconvenient places and under strange circumstances and for that I am greatly appreciative. I know he may have many more important people to work with and a very busy schedule to maintain. However I now understand why my father made him the executor of our trust - because he sees the value in me actually learning and understanding the trust so that I may use the resources for the intended purpose rather than just waste them on frivolous pleasure.

Over the years he has met my requests for impromptu meetings at my home, in his office and at times I'll just pick him up and we'll drive around and discuss the trust. Each time we meet my mind unfolds the layers, the depth of the provision and responsibility included within the trust. It is disappointing to me that I have taken such a long time to grasp the expanse of resource and responsibility outlined within the trust. To be honest there have been times I have hidden from the responsibility and not utilized the resource, probably for much the same reasons others would. I feel guilty because I was adopted into such a great trust and I don't feel worthy. At times I feel lazy and honestly just want to blend into the crowd.

I have an adopted daughter from Haiti who is now in her teens. We sometimes talk about our adoptions and the feelings that accompany it. My daughter Rose experiences many of the same emotions that I have, and as I watch her navigate those feelings it is an encouragement for me. There are days when she feels like she won the lottery, because she did. There are other days when she feels extreme guilt for those whom she left behind. There are days when she wants to just be "normal" and blend into the crowd rather than being a black girl in a wealthy white home in a southern community. She knows the purpose attached to the investment that Janelle, myself, our friends and family are making in her. That can be overwhelming at times but she is off to a better start than I was.

I met Rose when she was about seven years old when by chance I visited an island called La Goanve about 20 miles off the coast of Haiti. She had been found by the caretakers of the facility where I was staying, severely injured and abandoned. It took a year for the caretakers to nurse her back to health.

I visited La Gonave annually and began participating in some humanitarian work, mainly feeding children but the project expanded into drilling water wells. Nonetheless that isn't the topic for discussion here. With each trip I got to know Rose (my future adopted daughter). I looked at the conditions she lived in and the extreme hopelessness of the island where she lived. I knew that unless someone intervened she was destined for an early death from disease, no hope for a career, loving family or any sort of comfort at all.

I called my wife on the way home from work one day, very randomly, although things had been running through my head for quite sometime on the topic. I first called a friend, who now is a colleague of mine. Steve had been on some trips with me to La Gonave from which we have some incredible stories. But on this drive home I called Steve and told him I thought he should adopt Rose. He laughed and said I needed to.

Somewhere deep down I knew he was right. I was just learning to accept that. As I drove the next mile I called my attorney and asked his opinion. "Well you built that huge house and have some extra room. You seem capable of investing in her what she needs to be productive within your family. Your trust will support her as well." So I called my wife, not more than two miles later. I sat at a stoplight, dialed her number...

"Hi Janelle, I'm almost home, about 10 minutes away."

"Well, alright I'll see you then," she responded.

"Wait, let me ask you a question, what would you think about adopting Rose?" I asked her, very matter of factly.

"Well hon, I've been waiting on you." She responded in a much more direct tone.

I said "ok" and hung up, a little shocked but it shouldn't have surprised me at all. This is her way of doing things.

Janelle had never met Rose, only heard my stories from the previous two years. But she knows when something is the right thing to do. I tend to get really philosophical during decision-making. But today was a breakthrough for me, as it took all of five miles to talk to three people and make a very important life changing decision for us and for her. But that was all that went into the decision; we all knew it as the right thing to do.

The executor's patience in teaching me has now expanded for about 15 years. I am beginning to grasp the beginning from the end and believe the next book I write will be specifically about the trust and specifically how I have chosen to invest my portion. However for the time being it gets only a chapter in this writing.

The adoption process for Rose took approximately two years but we had no idea if it would have been six months (which we believed it would have been) or six years (as it felt like it turned into). I went back to La Gonave when we decided to adopt Rose and I told her Janelle and I were going to make her our daughter. I told her I would not see her again until I came to pick her up.

Traveling back through Port Au Prince I hired an attorney and used a liaison who navigated the dark corners of the Haitian government. Two years and thousands of dollars later we flew to Port Au Prince where Rose met us and we took her home.

The adoption process was difficult on our marriage, finances and home life, but we successfully and gratefully navigated it and began our new life with Rose. She will never fully understand the price we paid and continue to pay for her, and I accept that. It doesn't matter to me if she understands fully the sacrifice we made for her, rather she embraces the purpose she now has in life, does something great with it, and enjoys life along the way. We adopted her for her, not for us.

My father adopted me for me as well. I will never fully understand the price he paid for me, although I have tried, I now accept the fact that I cannot. I am fully embracing the outcome of the adoption rather than the process of it.

My adoption process took over three years and resulted in the brutal murder of my father's only naturally born son at the hands of a hostile government and jealous benefactors of the will and trust that was being enacted for many, I being one. That death showed my father's commitment to me when I wasn't even his child yet and for my lifetime will stand as a reflection of his unwavering commitment to me, even when I have failed the family.

Fortunately for me the trust is solely based on me being my father's son, and had absolutely nothing to do with my performance. I am not an employee of a corporation attempting to move up the corporate ladder and obtain great wealth. I was given all I ever need by my adopting father and I smugly admit that I get the benefits of the trust solely because my name is spelled out quite clearly on the dotted line. I can't earn it, I just had to accept the fact, whether I felt deserving or not, my father did, and he took great pleasure in giving me great opportunity in life.

Now that I have accepted that gift I have been able to move past my own insecurities and embrace the purpose of the trust. I accept the fact that I will be ridiculed frequently as others point out why I shouldn't have what I do but I have learned to tune that out and move forward.

My father didn't put a lot of requirements on me for personal behavior, or things I needed to do. There were only a few. But as I have continued conversing with my attorney about my father whom I never had the opportunity to meet face to face, I have changed as a person. What I want more than anything is to please him and represent my family to a standard that would make my father proud. Therefore, I deny myself many opportunities for pleasure that might taint his legacy as the giving, loving father he is.

As with any contract the one who holds the power controls the terms and conditions of the agreement. I've been on both ends of those contracts throughout my business career. Generally speaking the controlling end is the one you want to be on.

Fortunately for me when I started in business I had a very benevolent partner whom I have discussed in this book earlier. He could have taken advantage of me when funding PCI, but he didn't and he always treated me fairly. I think John reflected the attributes that I see in my father from a distance. He could have taken advantage of the situation but he didn't.

My father was the same way. He set some firm terms and conditions but he did it in my best interest and I chose to accept and embrace the terms and conditions.

The truth is my adopting father is the Lord himself. He wrote a last will and testament which contained many provisions for me to have a wonderful life. He then did the unthinkable and ratified the covenant with the blood of his own son Jesus Christ.

All religion tries to reach God through performance, and as human beings we cannot do that. It can be fun because some of us are more disciplined than others, so they feel more important or more religious. In fact we cannot reach God through trying to be like God.

God understood that so He provided an avenue for us to be adopted as His very own children, through the belief, acceptance and communication of the action that he took to ratify the covenant through Jesus Christ we can be adopted. Through that covenant Jesus, as first born son was given lordship of the family and control of the family business. Our acceptance of that lordship and submission to him brings us into a relationship with God himself, enjoy the benefits and run with the purpose of the trust.

If you want to read my trust I suggest reading the book of Hebrews found in the new testament. If you are a business guy it will make sense to you. I encourage and invite you into our family. Although we bicker like any family it's a loving bunch that will accept you as you are.

You have heard it said that one should not talk about money, religion or politics among friends. But I tell you those are not friends and probably not relationships worth keeping. At the end of this book I hope you see that I sincerely care about you as a person and more than that my father does. He asked me to write this book just so that he could personally contact you.

ABOUT THE AUTHOR

Eric English has followed an unorthodox path to success as most entrepreneurs do. After attending only one semester at a community college and two years at a technical school, he finished his first business plan at age 20. It took two years but he secured seed investment for Performance Composites Incorporated (PCI) start up funding.

PCI was profitable from year one and grew into an industry leader as an OEM and aftermarket supplier of composite products for the power sports industry. He steered the company through several growth cycles and sold half the company at age 30. Staying on as President, Eric navigated a diversification process that included the relocation of manufacturing to Mexico. In December 2005 PCI sold it's assets, and he left to pursue other ventures.

He has been happily married since 1996, to Janelle, who provides loving support that keeps him going. They live outside Tulsa, Oklahoma and find much enjoyment in raising their three children together.

Eric also serves at Guts Church in several capacities, primarily as an advisor. He also manages humanitarian relief programs for the island of La Gonave Haiti, which includes road work, water well drilling and other projects. He enjoys teaching on wealth through the Second Mile training program.

Currently Eric is expanding a chain of building supply stores with the most eccentric, fun and driven group of people he has ever worked with. Although he co-founded the business and serves as President, his business focus remains primarily on learning, teaching and understanding how to create and stimulate growth within organizations.

With an affinity toward motorcycle racing, Eric has also founded Synergy Motorsports. Although it is not his primary business pursuit, it remains an ongoing labor of love. www.synergymoto.com

Follow his weekly blog at www.eric-english.com where he continues to write about the lessons learned through his experiences in business, nonprofit work and life. Feel free to join the conversation.

If you would like to contact Eric English for consulting or speaking engagements, please e mail him through eric.h.english@gmail.com

Made in the USA
Charleston, SC
13 August 2010